YOUR EXPERT GUIDE

The Human Body for Young Scientists

LIAM CINI-O'DWYER AND TOM JACKSON
AND OLA SZPUNAR

Royal Society of Biology

First published in Great Britain in 2025 by Wayland
Copyright © Hodder & Stoughton 2025

All rights reserved.

Editors: Grace Glendinning and Julia Adams
Designer: Arvind Shah
Illustrator: Ola Szpunar

Produced in association with the Royal Society of Biology
www.rsb.org.uk

ISBN: 978 1 5263 2803 8 HBK
ISBN: 978 1 5263 2802 1 PBK
ISBN: 978 1 5263 2804 5 EBOOK

Printed and bound in Dubai

An imprint of
Hachette Children's Group
Part of Hodder & Stoughton
Carmelite House
50 Victoria Embankment
London EC4Y 0DZ

An Hachette UK Company
www.hachette.co.uk
www.hachettechildrens.co.uk

The authorised representative in the EEA is Hachette Ireland, 8 Castlecourt Centre, Castleknock Road, Castleknock, Dublin 15, D15 YF6A, Ireland
email: info@hbgi.ie

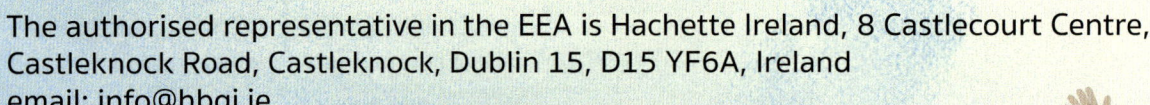

CONTENTS

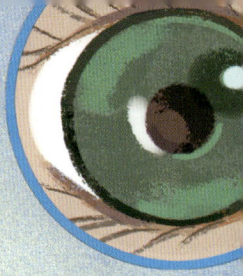

Foreword: Royal Society of Biology   4
Introduction: Welcome to the human body!   6

PART 1: What are humans made of?

Hello, everybody!   8
Building a body   10
Body systems   12
The skeleton   14
Muscle power   16
Muscles at work   18
Get some guts   20
Where does food go?   22
Know your teeth   24
The heart and blood   26
Take a breath   28
Brain and nervous system   30
Vision on   32
Listen, hear!   34
Taste and smell   36
The skin's super senses   38
Hair everywhere!   40

PART 2: How to stay healthy

Making healthy choices   42
Choose your foods   44
Keeping fit   46
Looking after your mental health   48
Infectious diseases   50
Being ill   52
Keep clean, stay healthy   54

PART 3: Growth

Growing up   56
Becoming an adult   58
Where babies come from   60

Glossary   62
Further information   63
Index   64

Welcome to the fascinating world of the human body.

Biology is the science of living things, from tiny cells to huge forests. It helps us understand how plants, animals and people grow, change and live together. This book is about human biology, which is the study of how our bodies work. From the microscopic bacteria inside our digestive systems, to the way our hearts beat and our brains think – learning about the human body helps us understand what makes us ... us!

The Royal Society of Biology wants to help people learn more about biology. We bring together scientists, teachers, students and anyone who is interested in the science of life. Our goal is to make learning about life exciting and useful for everyone.

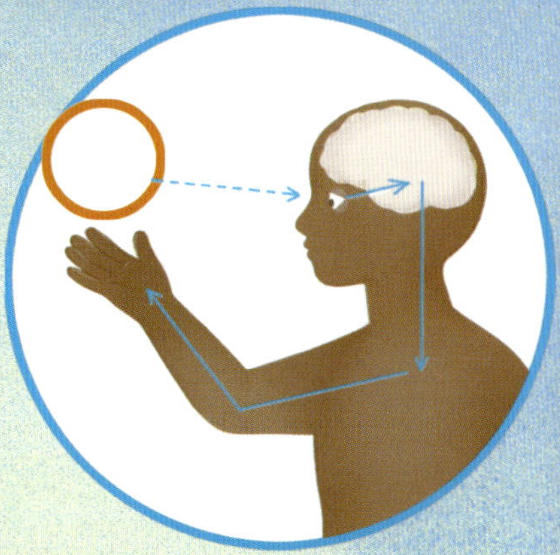

Young people are natural explorers! They love to ask questions, try new things and understand the world – just like professional scientists do. Science is a big part of our lives. It helps us make good choices about our health and our planet. By learning and observing, and by building on ideas we already understand, we can solve problems and make the world a better place. Science is for everyone, and anyone can take part in discovery.

We hope this book makes you curious, fills you with wonder and reminds you that learning never stops. Science is a great adventure, and you are part of it!

Dr Arianne Matlin

**Director of Policy and Publications
The Royal Society of Biology**

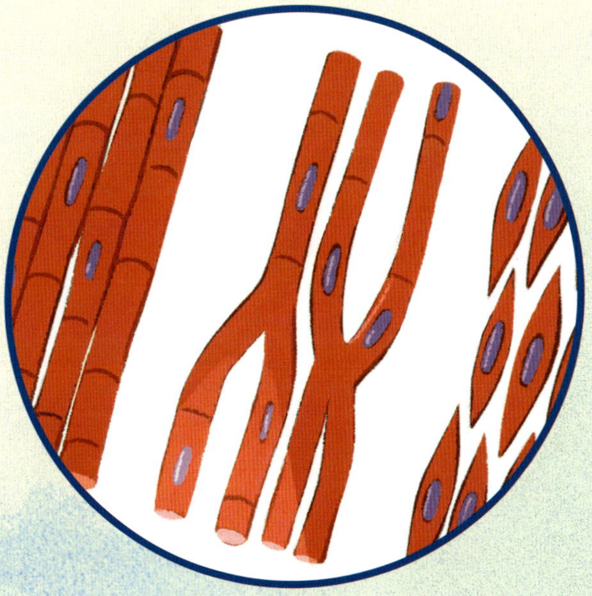

WELCOME TO THE HUMAN BODY!

Your body is part of what makes you YOU, so it makes good sense to get to know what is going on inside, what makes up your body and how it works. For example, did you know that you need muscles to see and bones to hear?

It's also important to explore how to look after your body, and how it might change as you get older. After all, you only have one body, and it is uniquely your own.

This book looks at all this and more!

Cells and systems

The first part of the book explores what the human body is made from. The body can be understood in different ways. It is made up of trillions of tiny building blocks, called cells. One body cell alone does not do much, but the cells work together to make powerful organs, such as the heart and lungs, and body systems like our skeleton.

Keeping healthy

Next, the book looks at how to keep your body healthy. This involves eating well, keeping active and looking after your feelings, too. And if you do become unwell, we'll show you how the human body is built to fight back.

Growing up ... and getting older

The final topic of the book is about where your body came from in the first place, and how it grew – and grew – to become you. What will it do next? You'll have to read on to find out!

I can't wait any longer! Let's take a tour of the human body!

HELLO, EVERYBODY!

Let's start off by having a look at the structure of your body and how it works. Learning about the structures of the body is called anatomy. Learning about how the body functions is called physiology.

Body parts

If you look at yourself in the mirror, you can see that you have a head on top of a neck, which comes out of the top portion of your torso, or what's called the thorax. Your arms come out of the sides of your thorax, at the shoulders.

The lower part of your torso, below the thorax and above your pelvis (see page 14), is called your abdomen.

Your legs then come out of the bottom of your pelvis.

If you can, turn around and you will see that you also have a backbone (also called a spine).

This means that you are a vertebrate. All vertebrate animals like you have a spine.

Hot and hairy

If you feel your skin, you should feel that you are giving off heat. This means that you are warm-blooded. This is a characteristic of being a type of vertebrate animal called a mammal. Along with being warm-blooded, mammals have hair or fur and breathe using a pair of lungs. Most give birth to live young (rather than laying eggs).

We are animals

Did you know that our closest living relatives are the chimpanzees, and that we are part of the same family as the other great apes, such as gorillas and orangutans? Along with them, we are part of a larger animal group called the primates.

Mammal hair comes in many different colours and textures.

BUILDING A BODY

Your body is made up of trillions (one trillion is a million millions) of tiny little building blocks, called cells. They are so small that you need a microscope to see them. Cells come in different shapes and sizes and have specific functions (jobs).

Cells make a body

Another name for a living thing is an organism. All organisms are made up of cells. Some organisms have a body made up of just one cell and are called unicellular. Organisms like us are made up of many cells, and are called multicellular.

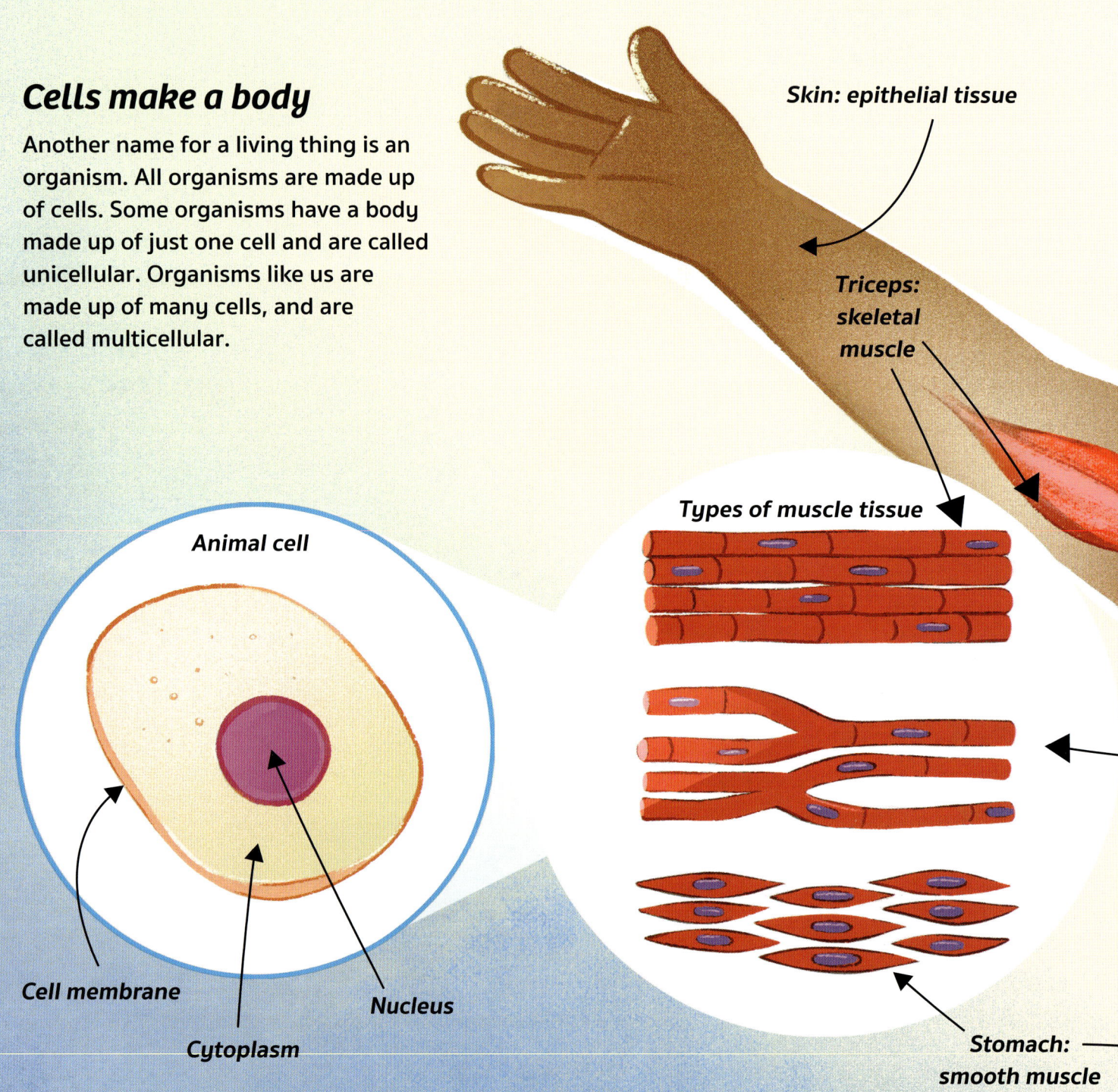

Skin: epithelial tissue

Triceps: skeletal muscle

Types of muscle tissue

Stomach: smooth muscle

Animal cell

Cell membrane

Nucleus

Cytoplasm

Tissue types

In a multicellular organism like you, groups of similar cells work together to perform a particular job for the body. These groups of cells are known as tissues. There are four basic types of tissue in humans:

- Nervous tissue, such as in the brain
- Connective tissue, such as bones
- Epithelial tissue, such as in the skin
- Muscle tissue, such as in your biceps.

Muscle tissue comes in three types: cardiac, skeletal and smooth, (see pages 16–17) and the other main tissues have many variations, too.

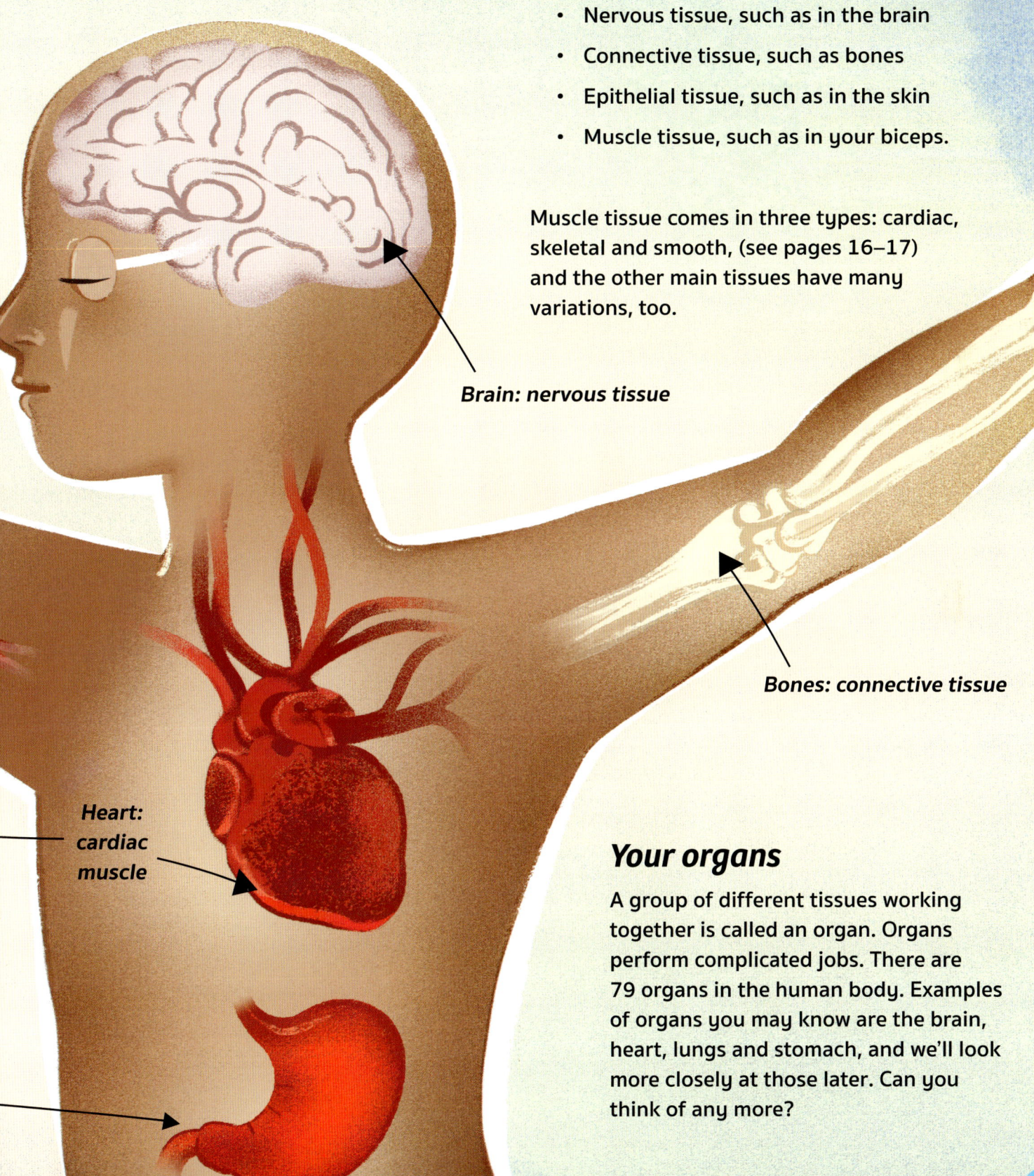

Brain: nervous tissue

Bones: connective tissue

Heart: cardiac muscle

Your organs

A group of different tissues working together is called an organ. Organs perform complicated jobs. There are 79 organs in the human body. Examples of organs you may know are the brain, heart, lungs and stomach, and we'll look more closely at those later. Can you think of any more?

BODY SYSTEMS

When groups of organs work together to carry out one or more functions, they are known as organ systems. How many organ systems do you think humans have if we have 79 organs?

Meet the team

The human body has 11 organ systems. You may have heard of some, and some have really complicated names. Which of the following have you heard of, and which ones sound unfamiliar?

Skeletal system: gives the body shape and support

Muscular system: moves the body

Digestive system: handles our food

Cardiovascular system: pumps blood around the body

Respiratory system: used for breathing

Lymphatic system: drains water from body tissues; removes germs

Remembering all those names

Often in biology, you will find that there are several different terms for the same thing. Organ systems are no exception.

For example, sometimes the cardiovascular system is called the circulatory system, and the respiratory system is also known as the breathing system. The lymphatic system can be called the immune system, and the urinary system is sometimes called the renal system.

Know the system

In this book, we are going to learn about six organ systems, their functions and the organs that make them up.

Can you come up with an easy way to remember the names of all 11 organ systems?

One way is by using this fun mnemonic:

*Silly Mice Do Cartwheels
Round New Roads Easily
Upsetting Lazy Iguanas*

Female reproductive system

Endocrine system: sends out chemical messages (hormones) that cause changes in the body

Reproductive system: Together, the female and male reproductive systems can produce offspring

Urinary system: removes waste as urine (wee)

Nervous system: controls the body's reaction to stimuli using bioelectrical signals

Integumentary system: skin, hair and nails

THE SKELETON

Some people might think skeletons are spooky, but we all have one inside us. Have you ever wondered what it is for? What do you think you would look like if you didn't have a skeleton holding you up? And what if all the bones of your skeleton were stuck together instead of being bendy at the joints?

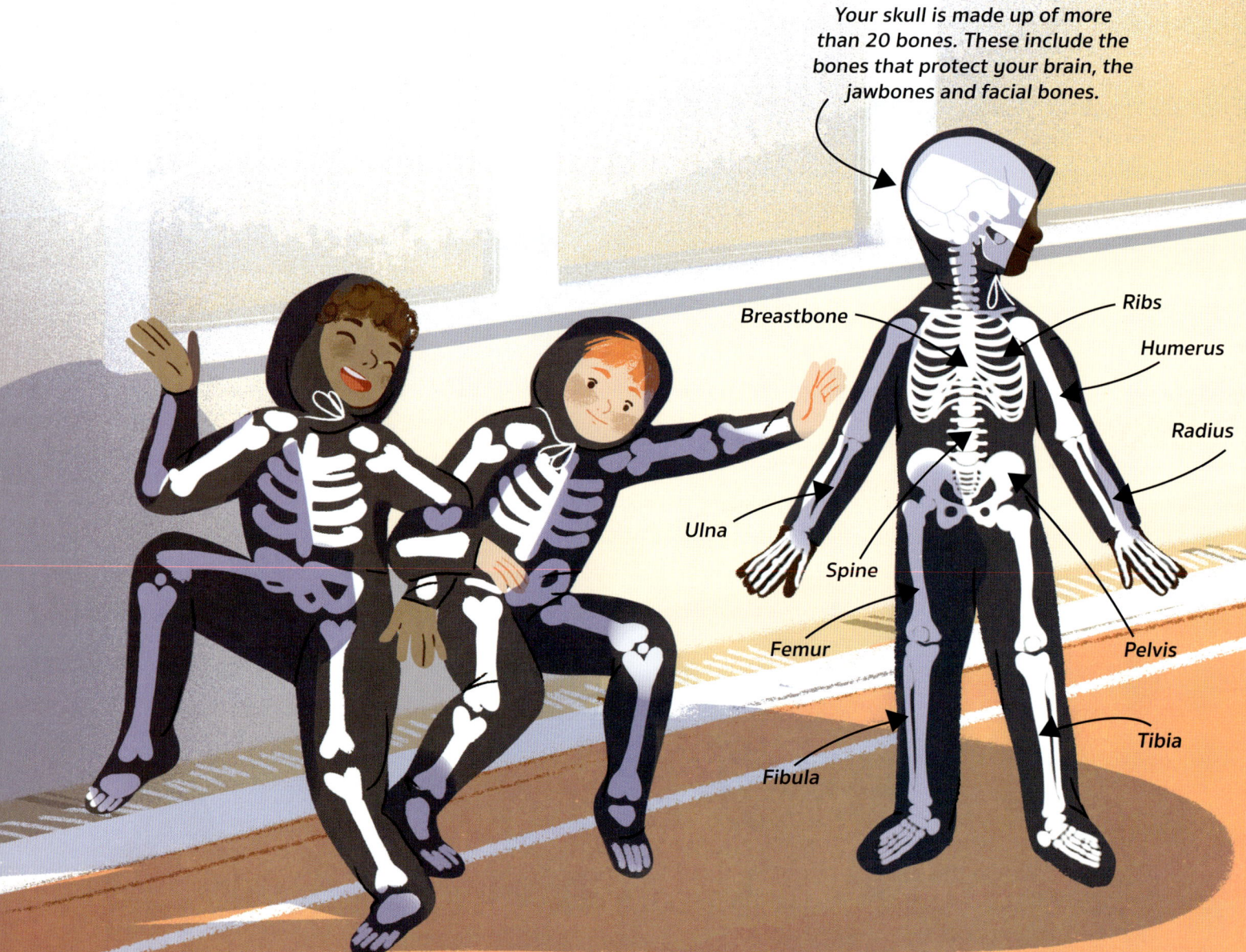

Your skull is made up of more than 20 bones. These include the bones that protect your brain, the jawbones and facial bones.

Shape up

The skeleton is part of the skeletal system – this includes our bones and everything that connects them together. The function of the skeletal system is to support the body and give it shape. It also protects the soft internal organs and allows the body to move at the joints.

14

Brilliant bones

Bones are a connective tissue that has been made hard and strong with a mineral called calcium phosphate. You are born with 270 bones but this decreases to 206 bones by adulthood because some of the bones fuse together!

Bones also store other minerals that your body needs. Even more amazing is that some of the bigger bones, such as the femur (thigh bone) and pelvis, actually make blood cells. More than 10 billion are made every day!

A hand has 27 bones. There are more bones in your hands and feet than in the rest of your body put together!

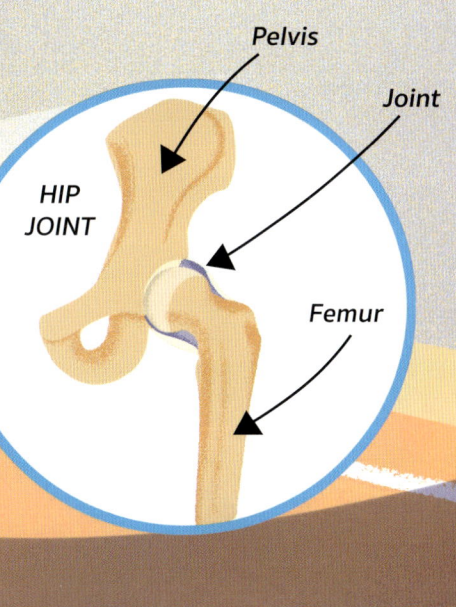

Jiggly joints

A joint is where two bones meet. The bones are connected by tough strings of slightly elastic tissue called ligaments. The ligaments hold the bones in place and make the joint sturdy, but still allow it to move.

If the joint bends the wrong way or twists too much, the ligament gets stretched. This is called a sprain. Sprains require that you rest the joint so the ligament can recover.

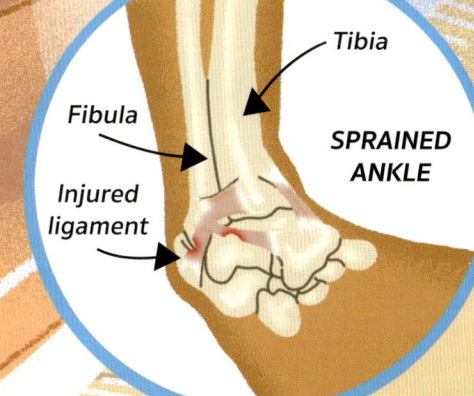

15

MUSCLE POWER

Muscles are the body's movers, lifters and shakers. They are found in the arms and legs, for example, but are also at work in most other parts of the body, from the eyes to the stomach to your blood vessels (see page 26). There are three types of muscle in the human body, and they all have a different job to do.

All action

Some of the functions of the muscular system are to allow the body to move, maintain posture and circulate blood around the body. However, it also helps in other things, such as breathing, giving birth and getting rid of waste (into the toilet)! Even when you are cold, it is your muscles that shiver to help you warm up.

Cardiac muscle tissue

One of the tissues that make up your heart organ is cardiac muscle tissue; it helps to make your heart beat, which pumps your blood around your body.

Smooth muscle tissue

Smooth muscle tissue is found in lots of places in your body, such as in the walls of most of your hollow organs, for example in the stomach, intestines and bladder. It's also in your airways, your blood vessels, your skin and even in your eyes!

Skeletal muscle tissue

Skeletal muscles move your skeleton so that you can move around. (You have control over these muscles, while the smooth and cardiac muscles work by themselves.) There are 640 skeletal muscles in the human body! Skeletal muscles are attached to the bones of your skeleton by cords of tough connective tissue, called tendons.

A muscle works by contracting (getting shorter) and relaxing. Contracting makes the tendon pull on the bone, and so the bone moves at the joint. When the muscle relaxes, it returns to its original length and the pulling stops.

MUSCLES AT WORK

Grab your upper left arm with your right hand. Slowly raise your left palm towards your left shoulder. Do you feel any changes in your upper arm? Which parts? Slowly lower your hand back down. Are there changes? Are they in the same place or somewhere else?

Working in pairs: arms

Skeletal muscles work together in pairs. These pairs do the opposite action of one another. So, as one muscle contracts, the other relaxes.

When you were raising and lowering your arm, you were feeling the muscle pair in your arm: the biceps in the front and the triceps in the back.

They work together to lift the lower arm (forearm) up and down, bending at the elbow joint. When the biceps contracts and the triceps relaxes, the forearm lifts. When the triceps contracts and the biceps relaxes, the lower arm moves downwards away from the shoulder, straightening the arm at the elbow.

Triceps muscle makes arm straight when it contracts

Biceps muscle bends arm when it contracts

Working in pairs: legs

Another example of skeletal muscles working in pairs to help you move are the quadriceps (quads) at the front of the thigh (upper leg) and hamstrings in the back of the thigh. These muscles contract and relax to move the lower leg forwards and backwards at the knee joint.

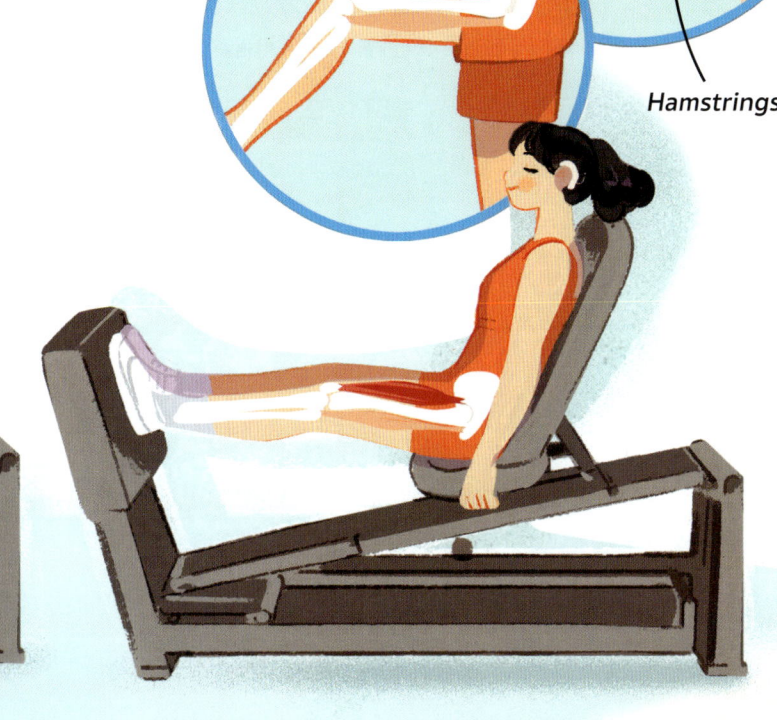

Step by step

Walking is a full-body workout, because it requires muscles from all over the body. For those who can walk, learning it takes a lot of trial and error. Babies typically learn to walk between the ages of 9 and 18 months. It can take many weeks or even months for them to figure out how to coordinate all those muscles to work together.

GET SOME GUTS

Have you ever wondered where your food goes once you have eaten it? Or why you need to eat at all? You need to eat because you need the nutrients in your food to give you energy, to help you grow and to stay healthy. Later we will consider what makes up a healthy diet, but first let's have a look at the structure and function of the digestive system.

Food supply

The digestive system's function is to break down food (digest it) into tiny particles, so that they can be absorbed into the body's bloodstream and travel to where they are needed. These nutrients are then used by the body's cells to keep the body healthy and functioning.

Nutrients also provide energy for growth, repair, warmth and movement. Food that cannot be broken down (such as fibre) is not absorbed. It moves through to the end of the digestive system and is released as faeces (poo).

Hidden tube

The digestive system is a long tube (tract) connecting the mouth to the anus, with many twists and turns along the way. An adult's digestive tract is about 9 m long end to end. It needs to be this long so that your food has time to be digested and absorbed into the body as it passes through.

Break it down

There are two types of digestion: mechanical and chemical. Mechanical digestion is when large food particles are chopped up into smaller pieces. Chewing with your teeth is an example of this.

Chemical digestion occurs when liquids are released to break down the large food molecules and split them up into smaller parts. These chemicals are called digestive enzymes. There are some in your saliva and stomach acid, but most are found in your small intestines and are produced by the pancreas.

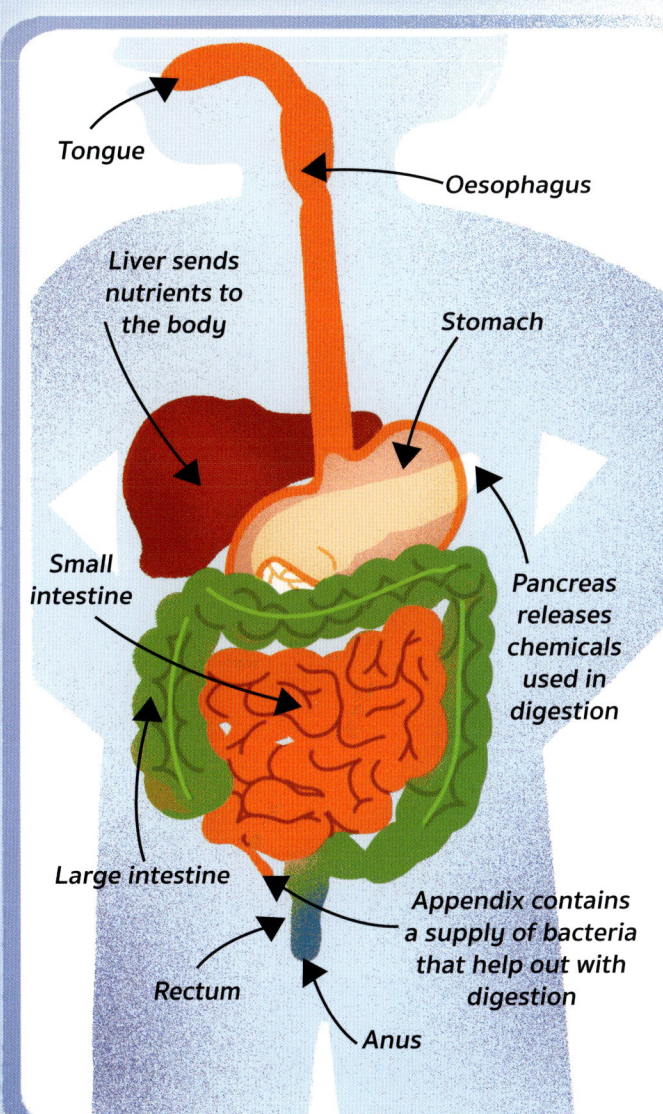

Tongue

Oesophagus

Liver sends nutrients to the body

Stomach

Small intestine

Pancreas releases chemicals used in digestion

Large intestine

Appendix contains a supply of bacteria that help out with digestion

Rectum

Anus

Follow food from mouth to toilet on the next page!

WHERE DOES FOOD GO?

We all know about eating food. We do it every day. And we all know where the leftovers end up – in the toilet! But what happens in between? Follow the food to find out.

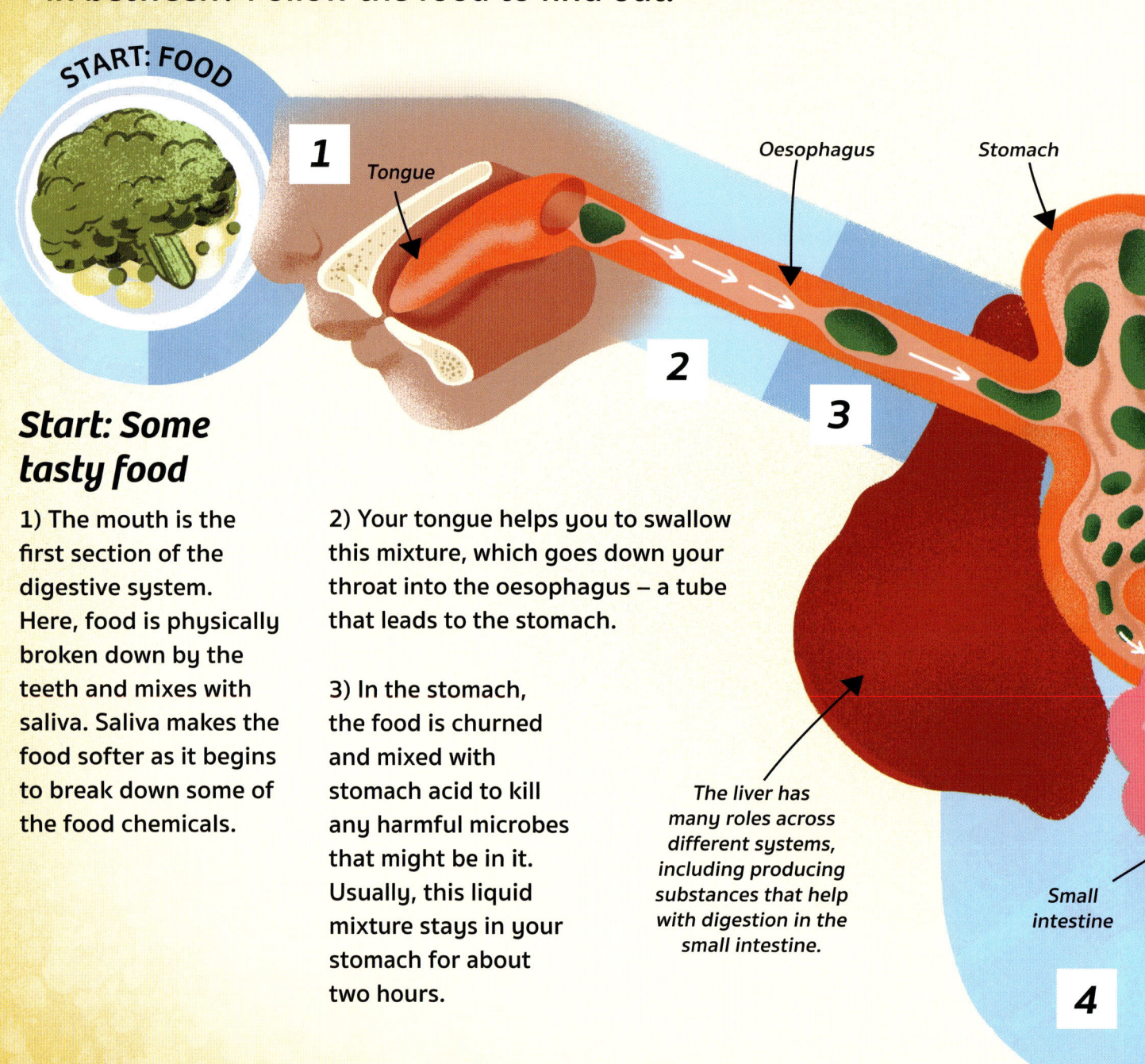

The liver has many roles across different systems, including producing substances that help with digestion in the small intestine.

Start: Some tasty food

1) The mouth is the first section of the digestive system. Here, food is physically broken down by the teeth and mixes with saliva. Saliva makes the food softer as it begins to break down some of the food chemicals.

2) Your tongue helps you to swallow this mixture, which goes down your throat into the oesophagus – a tube that leads to the stomach.

3) In the stomach, the food is churned and mixed with stomach acid to kill any harmful microbes that might be in it. Usually, this liquid mixture stays in your stomach for about two hours.

4) The food mixture enters the small intestine, where it is chemically broken down further and pushed along. This usually takes around five hours. Most of the digestion of your food happens here, in the small intestine.

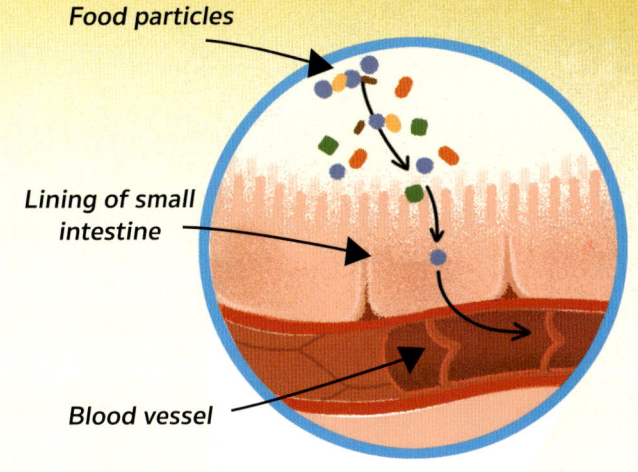

5) By now, the food has been split up into really small and simple parts. These are small enough to pass through the wall of the small intestine to be absorbed into the bloodstream. They then travel around to the other parts of the body where they are needed. Anything in the food that can't be broken down remains in the small intestine.

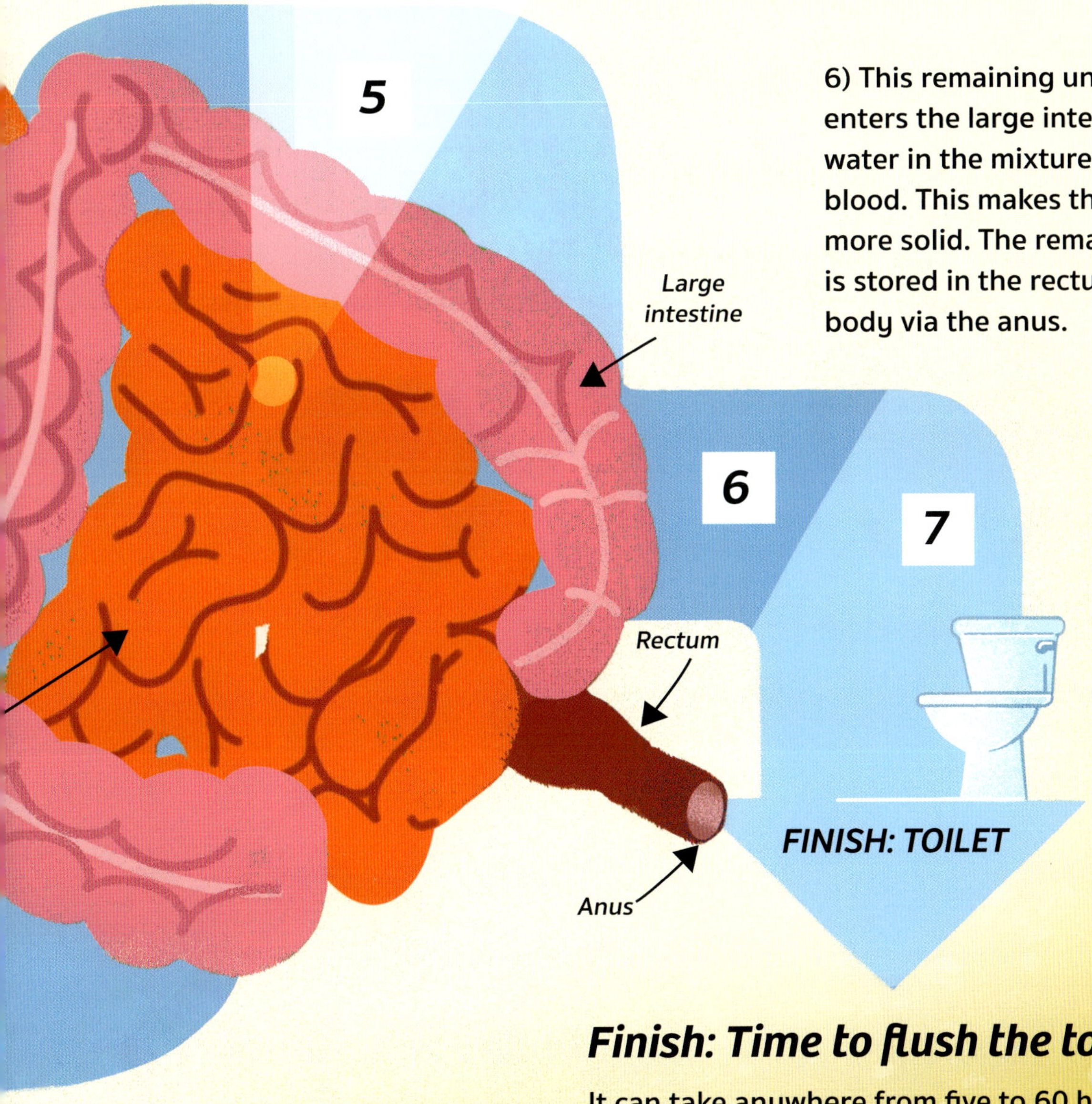

6) This remaining undigested food then enters the large intestine, where any water in the mixture is absorbed into the blood. This makes the undigested food more solid. The remaining waste material is stored in the rectum and exits the body via the anus.

7) The faeces passes out of the body when you defaecate (use the toilet).

FINISH: TOILET

Finish: Time to flush the toilet!

It can take anywhere from five to 60 hours for the mixture to move through just the small intestine. This means that the whole digestive process, from the time you swallow food to the time it leaves your body, can be between two and five full days (48–120 hours)!

KNOW YOUR TEETH

Have you ever wondered what your teeth are, or what they are made of? Are they bones? Although they seem similar, teeth are not bones and, unlike bones, they can't repair themselves if broken.

What are teeth?

Teeth are made of layers of hard tissue called enamel, dentine and root cement. In the centre of the tooth is soft, living tissue, called pulp. One important function of teeth is to physically break down food by cutting and crushing it, so that the food particles are small enough to swallow.

Humans have four types of teeth

Incisors are at the front. They have a thin edge used for biting and slicing chunks off food.

Canines are the fang-like, pointed teeth. They are good for gripping food as you bite.

Premolars and molars are wider, flatter teeth. They are used for grinding the food.

Teeth sit in the gums, the fleshy tissue covering the bones of the jaw.

Adults typically have 32 teeth. The top and bottom jaws each have four incisors, two canines, four premolars and six molars.

Teeth for life

Humans develop two whole sets of teeth. The first set is called baby teeth, or milk teeth. There are usually 20 of these and they start to appear when babies are around six months old (and getting ready to eat solid food). This period is called teething, and it can be painful for the baby, as the gums can become swollen and tender. Baby teeth are known as deciduous, because they fall out throughout childhood as the second set of teeth emerges.

The second set is the permanent, adult teeth. There are 32 of them.

Brushing your teeth

These adult teeth should last the rest of our life, if we keep the teeth and gums clean. So, it is important to brush your teeth twice a day.

It is also very important not to drink fizzy or sugary drinks too often. Sugar feeds bacteria that cause decay (holes) in teeth, and acid in fizzy drinks (even sugar-free ones) weakens the enamel, which can't regrow.

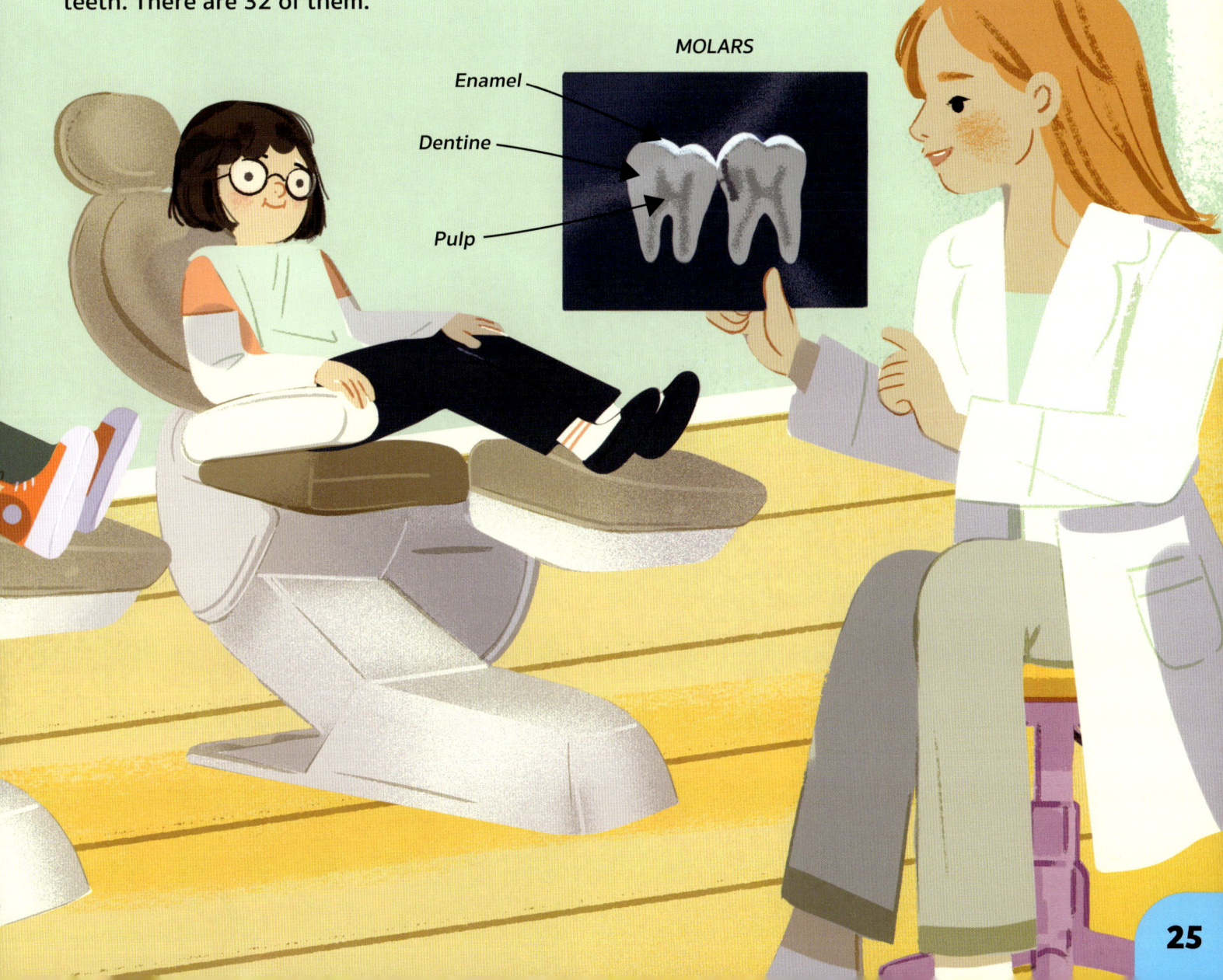

MOLARS
Enamel
Dentine
Pulp

THE HEART AND BLOOD

The cardiovascular system is sometimes known as the circulatory system because it circulates blood. From your heart, the blood travels through a network of tubes, called blood vessels, which reach every part of the body. Blood carries nutrients, water, oxygen and other important chemicals to help your body parts function.

Your beating heart

Your heart is a muscular pump that has the job of pushing blood around the body. Each push is called a heartbeat. The left side of the heart pushes some of the blood to the lungs to pick up a fresh supply of oxygen from the air you breathe in. The right side of the heart has the job of pumping blood around the rest of the body.

You can feel your heartbeat when you feel the pulse on the underside of your wrist. It beats around 60–110 times per minute when you are resting, but can go much, much faster when your body is working hard.

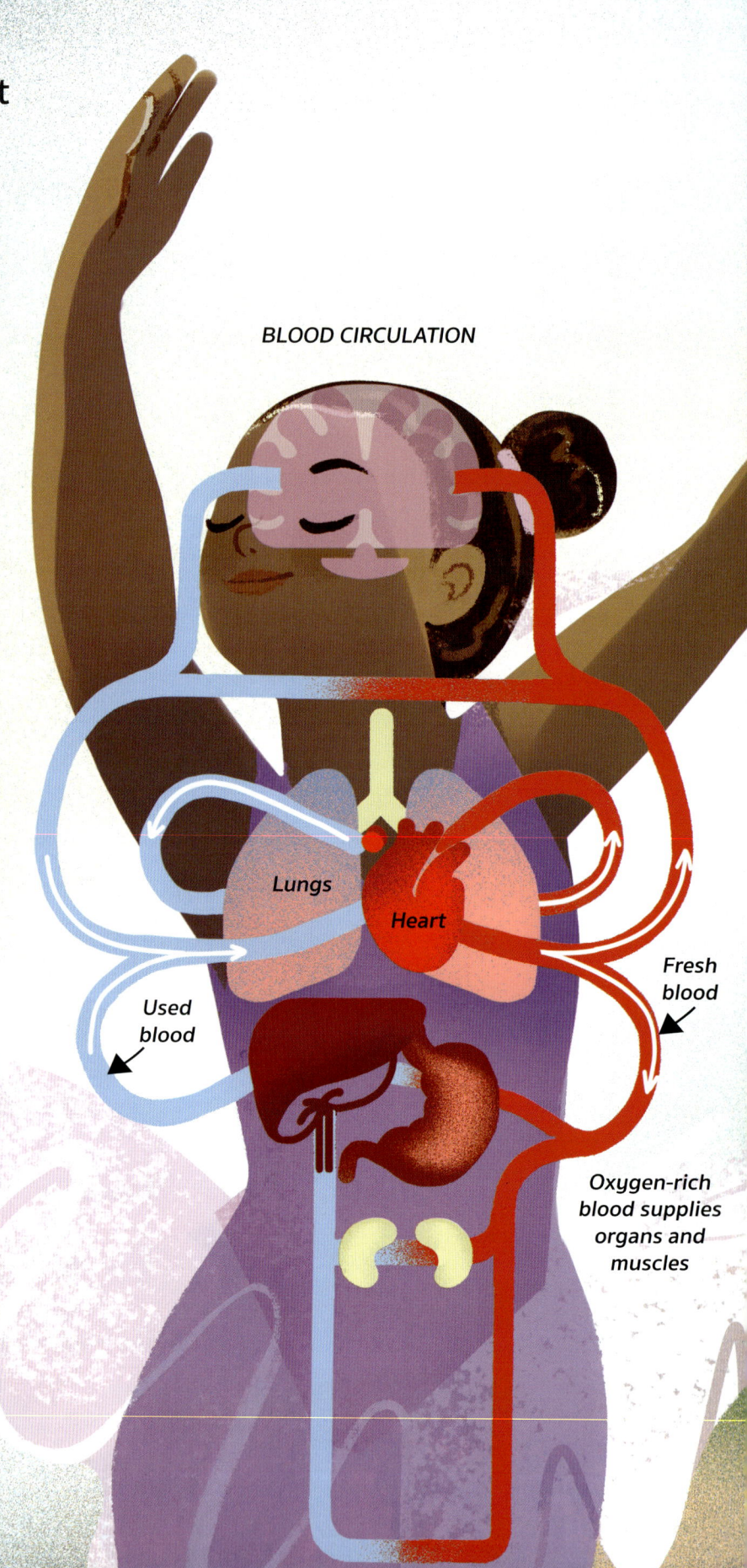

BLOOD CIRCULATION

Lungs
Heart
Used blood
Fresh blood
Oxygen-rich blood supplies organs and muscles

Blood cells

Blood is a mixture of liquid and cells. Most of the cells – there are many billions of them – are red-coloured. The red comes from a chemical called haemoglobin that absorbs (soaks up) oxygen. When oxygen combines with haemoglobin, it turns bright red. The red blood cells transport oxygen around the body to wherever it is needed.

The blood then picks up the waste gas carbon dioxide from the body's cells. The red blood cells then go back to the lungs to remove the carbon dioxide and get more oxygen (from air inhaled into the lungs).

RED BLOOD CELLS

Blood vessels

There are three kinds of blood vessels.

Arteries transport blood away from the heart to the capillaries.

Capillaries are tiny vessels that carry blood into and out of the body's organs and tissues, giving away oxygen and collecting waste, such as carbon dioxide and urea.

Veins then carry blood from the capillaries back to the heart. Some veins run close to the skin and look a bit blue due to the tissue they are made up of. The blood inside is dark red, as it does not have much oxygen in it.

TAKE A BREATH

The breathing system is also called the respiratory system. Its main function is, well, breathing (also called ventilation). This process exchanges oxygen gas from the air for carbon dioxide gas made by the body.

Feel the air

Put your hands on your chest and take a big breath in and out. What do you feel? Now place your hands on the sides of your ribs and, again, take a big breath in and out. What do you feel?

Wrap your arms around yourself and try to place your hands on the upper part of your back if you can (you might need to bend forward a bit). Take a big breath in and out. What happens?

You should find that when you breathe in, your chest, sides and upper back expand upwards and outwards. When you breathe out, they contract downwards and inwards.

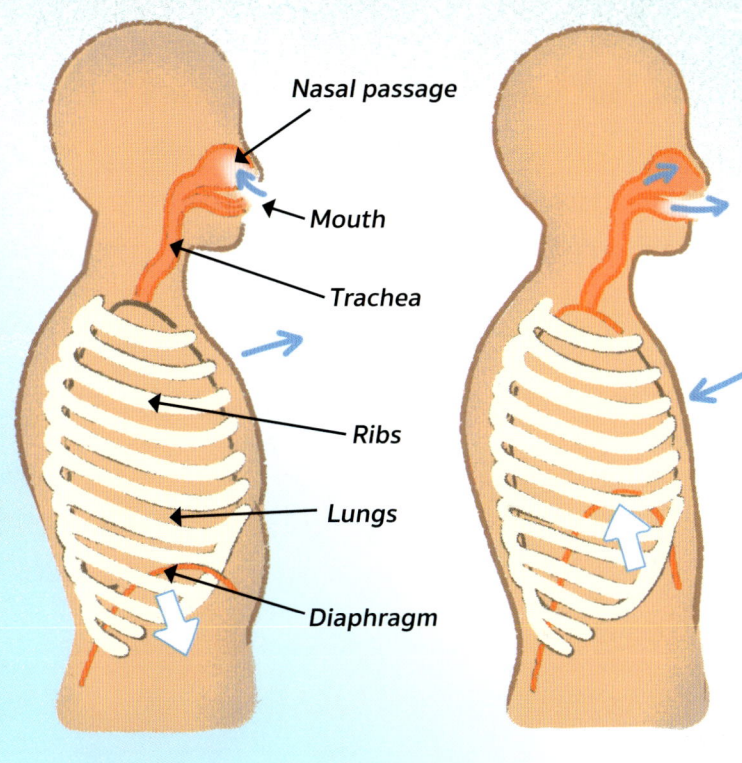

BREATHING IN   BREATHING OUT

Muscles and breathing

Muscles between and below the ribs (intercostal muscles and the diaphragm) contract and relax to change the volume (size) of the space inside your thorax, which enables the lungs to inflate and deflate, allowing you to ventilate.

In and out

When you breathe in (inhale), you deliver oxygen from the air to the bloodstream. When you breathe out (exhale), you remove carbon dioxide from your body to the air. As we saw earlier, the heart then beats to pump the oxygenated blood around the body to where it is needed.

The oxygen is used in a process inside the body's cells, called respiration. This is when our cells release energy by reacting sugar with oxygen. This energy is then used to help our cells to function.

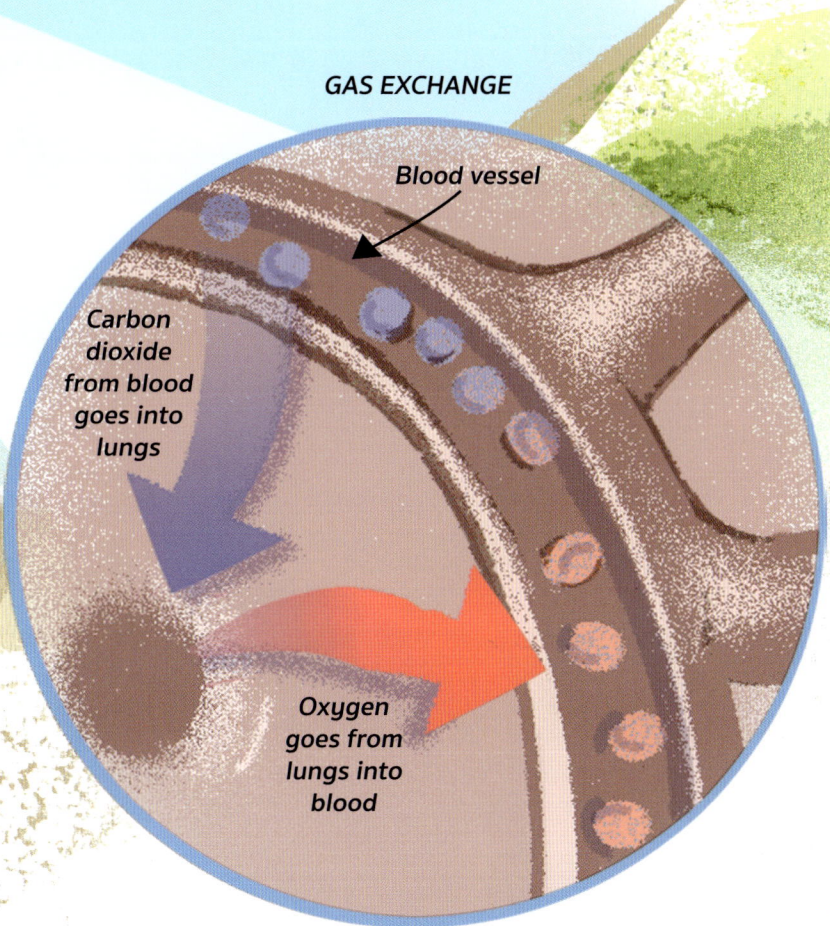

GAS EXCHANGE

The leftovers

Waste products from respiration are carbon dioxide and water. These are released by the body's cells back into the bloodstream. The carbon dioxide is delivered to your lungs, where you remove it by exhaling. You need to remove carbon dioxide from your body by breathing it out because it is toxic at high concentrations in your blood.

BRAIN AND NERVOUS SYSTEM

The nervous system is made up of the brain, spinal cord, nerves and sense organs, such as your eyes, ears and nose. The function of the nervous system is to collect information from the senses and then organise what the body will do next.

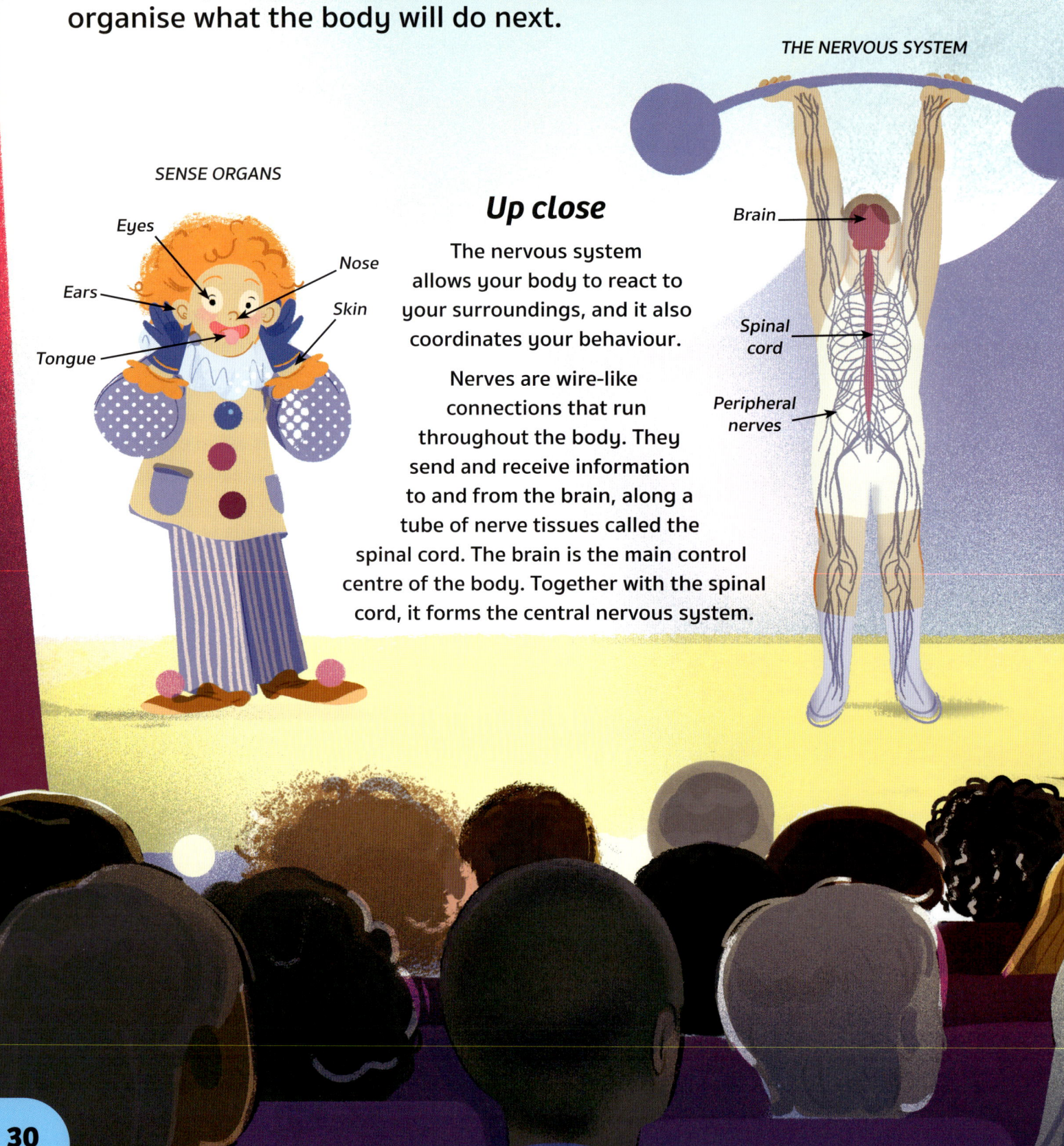

SENSE ORGANS
- Eyes
- Ears
- Nose
- Tongue
- Skin

THE NERVOUS SYSTEM
- Brain
- Spinal cord
- Peripheral nerves

Up close

The nervous system allows your body to react to your surroundings, and it also coordinates your behaviour.

Nerves are wire-like connections that run throughout the body. They send and receive information to and from the brain, along a tube of nerve tissues called the spinal cord. The brain is the main control centre of the body. Together with the spinal cord, it forms the central nervous system.

Neurones at work

Nerves are made of cells called neurones, which come in many interesting shapes. Some look like many-tentacled sea monsters! Others are long and thin with many branches.

When a nerve has a message to send, it creates a pulse of electricity that whizzes through the neurone. This is the fastest way to carry signals through the body.

A NEURONE TRANSMITTING AN IMPULSE

Signal arrives here

Electrical pulse moves along the neurone

Signal passes to next neurone

Fast worker

It is this fast, responsive communication system that allows you to:

- detect changes in the environment (a stimulus) with your sensory organs (e.g. hear a loud bang)
- send the information to your brain
- process the information in your brain
- send the information to an effector (something that carries out an action) in your body, such as your muscles, and have some sort of response to that stimulus (e.g. contraction, making you jump up).

Stimulus

Brain

Effector

VISION ON

Your eyes are sphere-like organs that help you see. Light enters your eye through an opening in the front, called the pupil. The pupil is surrounded by the iris, which can change shape to make the opening bigger or smaller allowing more or less light into the eye.

Making pictures

A muscle makes the lens change shape to focus the light onto the back of the eye. There, we have a light-sensitive tissue called the retina. The retina then creates an electrical impulse and sends this signal along the optic nerve to the back of your brain. The brain processes the information and makes sense of it. This is how you see.

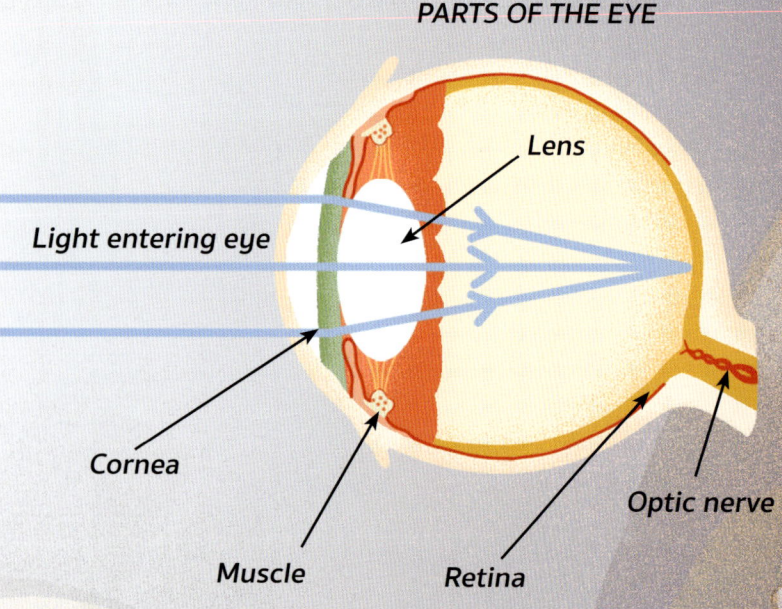

PARTS OF THE EYE

- Light entering eye
- Cornea
- Muscle
- Lens
- Retina
- Optic nerve

Visual impairment

Visual impairment is the partial or total inability to see, because part of the eye, the optic nerve or the part of the brain that deals with vision, may not be functioning. A person who is severely sight-impaired is considered to be blind.

Sight variations

Roughly one in four people have a problem with focusing light on to the retina. This is often due to an irregularly shaped eyeball. These difficulties mean that a person's vision is blurred. This can cause a person to be far-sighted or short-sighted. Both can be corrected with glasses or contact lenses to make sure light rays are correctly focused on the retina.

Eyelid

Pupil

Iris

LISTEN, HEAR!

When an object moves, it makes the air around it vibrate and generate a sound wave. These sound waves spread out in all directions and are picked up by our ears.

How it works

Your outer ear (called the pinna) funnels sound waves into your ear canal.

Inside the ear canal is the eardrum. When the sound wave hits the eardrum, it creates vibrations. The vibrations are sent to three tiny bones called the hammer, anvil and stirrup. These tap out a pattern on a spiral-shell-shaped structure called the cochlea. The tapping makes ripples in the liquid that's inside the cochlea.

These ripples are processed by the auditory nerve, which sends electrical signals to the brain – and we hear a sound!

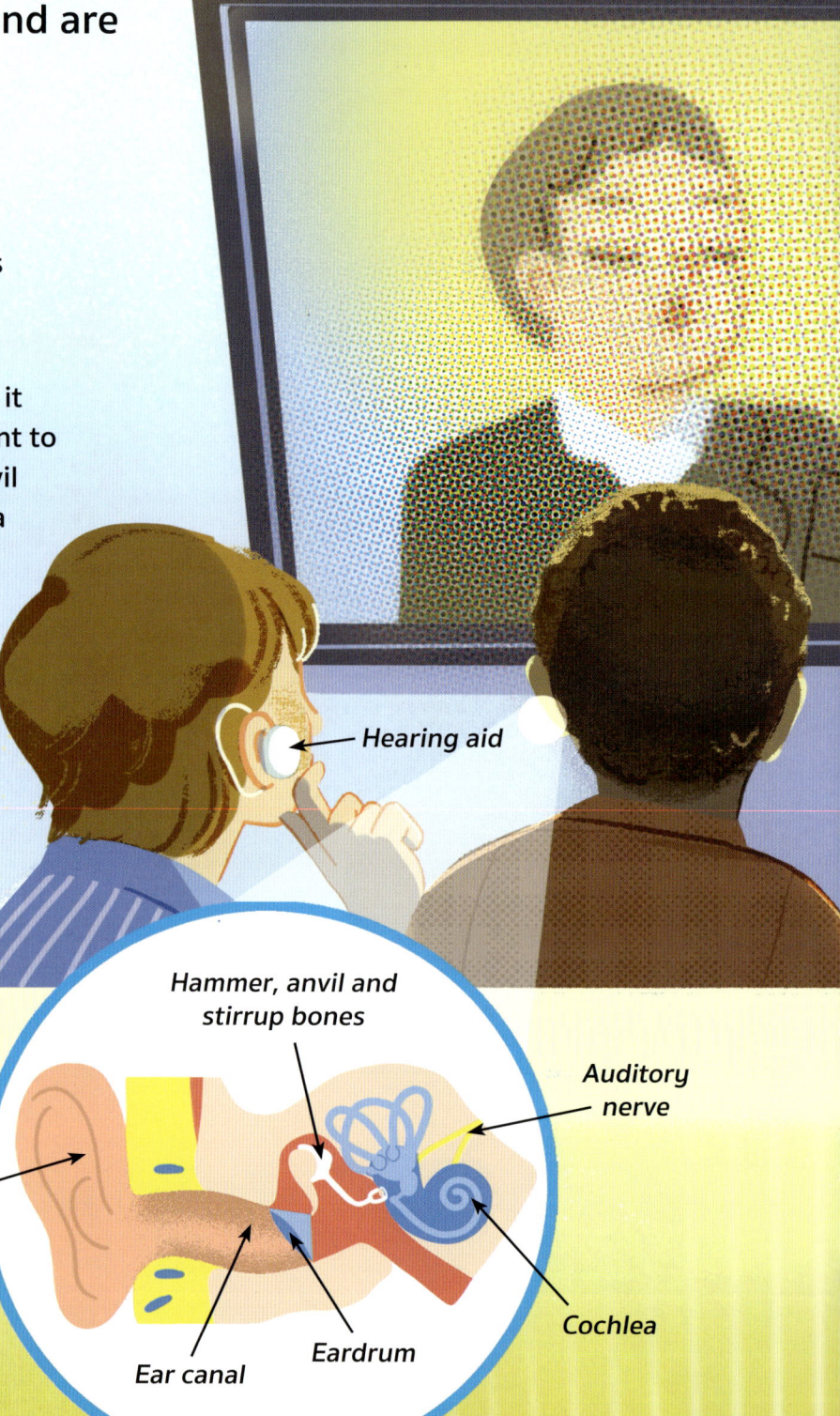

Hearing loss

Hearing loss is the partial or total inability to hear, because part of the ear, the auditory nerve or the part of the brain that deals with sound, is not functioning. Roughly one in eight people will have some form of hearing loss at some point in their life.

Deafness is when a person is unable to hear speech, even if it is loud. Deaf people tend to communicate in sign language as their first language. A person with partial hearing loss may wear hearing aids to help them hear.

Cleaning system

Earwax helps to keep our ears clean. It is an oily or flaky substance that can be brown, orange, red or yellow. It traps dirt that gets in the ear and also contains chemicals that help to prevent any infections. The wax will naturally fall out and take the dirt with it.

Ear defenders can help reduce noise for those with sensitive hearing

Looking after your ears

You should never stick anything in your ear canal because the eardrum is very delicate, so you don't want to pierce it. Also, don't listen to music that is too loud, especially on headphones, because you can permanently damage the inner parts of the ear.

TASTE AND SMELL

If you look in the mirror and stick out your tongue, can you touch the tip of your nose with it? Only about one in ten people can do this. The tongue can move like this because it is a muscle. It is really important in helping you eat, drink, speak and taste. It also helps to keep your teeth clean.

Tasty!

You can taste food because taste buds on your tongue detect the different chemicals in what you eat. There are thousands of taste buds on your tongue. Taste buds detect sweetness, sourness, saltiness, bitterness and savouriness (also called umami). They generate an electrical signal that is sent through nerves to your brain, which interprets the information. This is how you sense taste.

A supertaster is someone whose sense of taste is much more sensitive than most people's.

Ageusia (pronounced ag-you-zee-uh) is when someone has lost their sense of taste. Ageusia is relatively rare. However, cases have increased recently as it can be a symptom of a COVID-19 infection.

Lip

Taste buds

Tongue

Taste buds

36

Getting nosy

Your nose is a really important part of your breathing system. However, it is also used for your sense of smell.

You can smell something because chemicals in the air enter your nose. These dissolve in the mucus – or snot – in your nose, and smell sensors detect them. The sensors generate an electrical signal that is sent along the olfactory nerve to your brain for it to interpret. This is how you detect all the different smells.

Anosmia (pronounced an-oz-mee-uh) is the loss of the sense of smell or the inability to detect one or more smells. It could be permanent or only temporary, such as when you have a blocked nose. Without smell, food does not taste the same. It turns out that we smell food as we eat it, and that helps enhance its flavours.

THE SKIN'S SUPER SENSES

The skin is your largest organ. It is your body's outer covering and it does a huge number of jobs. It stops germs getting inside, and prevents your body parts from falling out!

In layers

Skin has three main layers. The top layer is the epidermis, which is made of dead cells. New epidermis cells are made by the middle layer, called the dermis. The bottom layer, the hypodermis, is a layer of fatty tissue.

Touch sensors

Among the skin cells are many sensors. Together they create the sense of touch. They each detect a particular sensation: hot and cold; hard pressure; soft touch; sharp pricks.

Controlling temperature

The skin also works to keep us warm and cool us down. When we are hot, the blood vessels underneath get wider, allowing more blood to flow under the skin, so more of the body's heat is lost to its surroundings. Sweat glands pump sweat onto the skin, and your body heat causes the water in the sweat to evaporate, which cools you down.

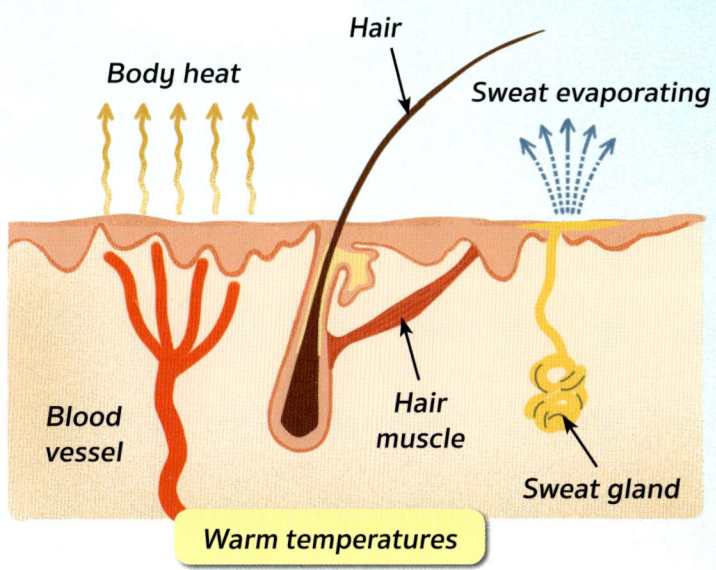

Warm temperatures

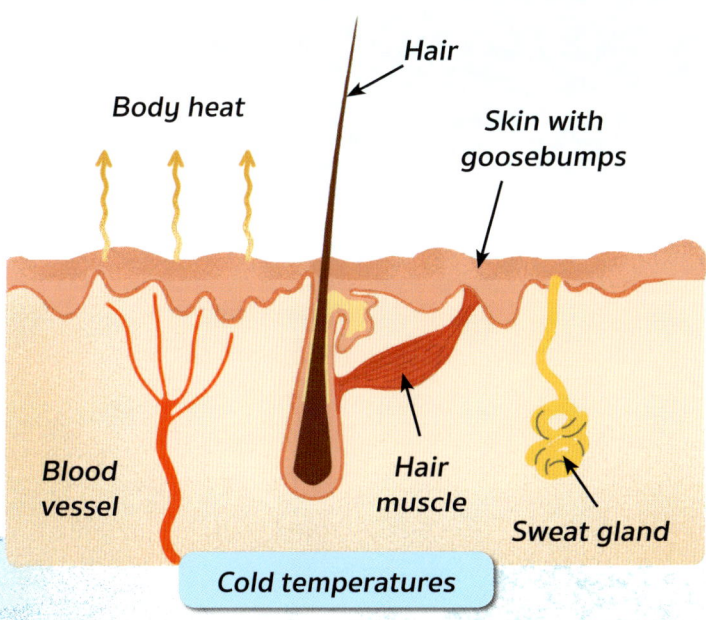

Cold temperatures

When it is cold, the blood vessels underneath the skin get narrower, so less blood flows to the surface of the skin. This means less heat is lost. Smooth muscle in the dermis makes the hairs stand up, creating little 'goosebumps.' The hairs work like a blanket to trap heat, keeping you warmer.

Protecting the skin

When your skin is exposed to sunlight, it makes a chemical called vitamin D, which your body needs to make strong bones, keep you healthy and fight off infection.

Did you know that your skin also helps protect itself by making a natural sunscreen called melanin? People who have more melanin in their skin have a darker skin tone. Despite this, every skin tone needs extra protection from the Sun. Seek shade, cover your skin and regularly top up your sunscreen!

HAIR EVERYWHERE!

Have a look in the mirror at the hair on top of your head. Is it all one colour? How long and thick is each hair? Do you have curly, wavy or straight hair? Or maybe you have no hair at all? There are a lot of varieties of hair!

What is hair?

Hairs are fibres that grow out of hair follicles in the skin. The part of the hair in the follicle is called the bulb, or root. The part of the hair that grows out of the skin is called the shaft. This is the part you can see. Hair is made of dead cells.

Follicles secrete an oil called sebum onto the hair to stop it drying out. Hair is made mostly from a flexible and waterproof chemical called keratin. In general, thicker hair grows faster (11 mm per month) than thinner hair (8 mm per month).

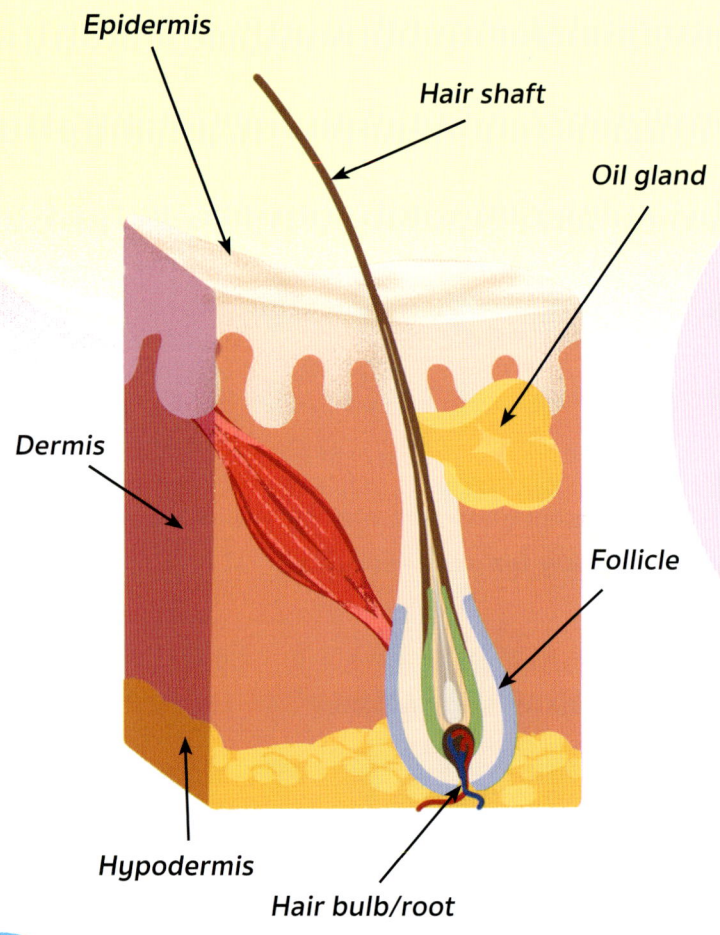

Did you know that fingernails are made of keratin? Keratin also makes up things such as animals' feathers, hooves and horns.

Why is my hair this colour?

All hair colours are formed by two types of coloured chemicals, or pigments. Black and brown hair mostly has a darker pigment, called eumelanin. Red hair has mostly pheomelanin. Blonde hair has low levels of both eumelanin and pheomelanin. Grey hair occurs when pigmentation levels drop. White hair has no pigmentation at all.

HAIR PIGMENTATION

Pheomelanin

Eumelanin and pheomelanin

Eumelanin

Why is my hair straight or curly?

The shape of a follicle makes the hair grow straight or in curls. Round follicles make straight hair and curved follicles make hair curly or coily. Wavy hair comes from having egg-shaped follicles.

Hair loss

Losing patches of hair from the head or body is called alopecia or baldness. It could be from a very small area to the entire body. Some of the main causes are related to ageing, genetics or changes in some hormone levels. It can be temporary or permanent.

MAKING HEALTHY CHOICES

A balanced diet can positively affect physical and mental health. So, eating different types of foods is important. For example, have you ever heard the advice to 'eat the rainbow'? This means by eating vegetables and fruits of different colours of the rainbow, you are very likely to receive a good range of minerals and vitamins for maintaining health and wellbeing.

Know your nutrients

The useful chemicals in food are called nutrients. Macronutrients (sometimes called macros) are the nutrients your body needs in large amounts. These are proteins, complex carbohydrates and healthy fats. They help to maintain your body's systems and structures.

Fruits and vegetables

BEANS

NUTS

Protein

Micronutrients (sometimes called micros) are equally as important, but are consumed in smaller amounts. These are vitamins and minerals. They help to keep your organs functioning and your cells healthy.

Variety is the spice of life

Each type of food has different quantities of these macro- and micro-nutrients. So, it is important to eat a range of healthy foods to make sure you are getting the correct balance of nutrients. For example, children and teenagers grow rapidly and have high energy requirements. This needs to come from nutritious food in regular meals to give you energy and nutrients to grow well and stay healthy.

Carbohydrates

Dairy and dairy alternatives

Oils and spreads

Eat your greens!

Some of our food is not used by the body, but that does not mean it is not healthy. These leftover substances are called fibre. Green vegetables are full of this stuff – and everyone knows they are good for you! Fibre passes through the digestive system more or less unchanged. However, along the way it gives the muscles in the stomach and intestines a good workout, so they stay strong. Regular workouts for your intestines keep your digestion moving along at a healthy rate.

CHOOSE YOUR FOODS

Have you heard the expression, "You are what you eat"? That makes sense because your body is built from the nutrients in your food, so make sure you are getting everything you need. Your meals should contain these five kinds of food to fuel your body:

Complex carbohydrates

These give you energy and are best found in wholegrain foods, such as bread, pasta, rice and cereals. Oats, quinoa and potatoes (with their skin on) are good, too.

Vegetables and fruits

These are important for providing vitamins and minerals. They also contain some carbohydrates for energy and are a good source of dietary fibre. Leafy green vegetables, such as cabbage and spinach, are especially nutritious. So, make sure to eat up your greens, such as broccoli, sprouts, peas, green beans and cauliflower.

Protein and iron-rich foods

These are important to help you to grow and make new cells. Good sources of these are lean meat, fish, eggs, nuts, pulses (such as beans and lentils) and tofu.

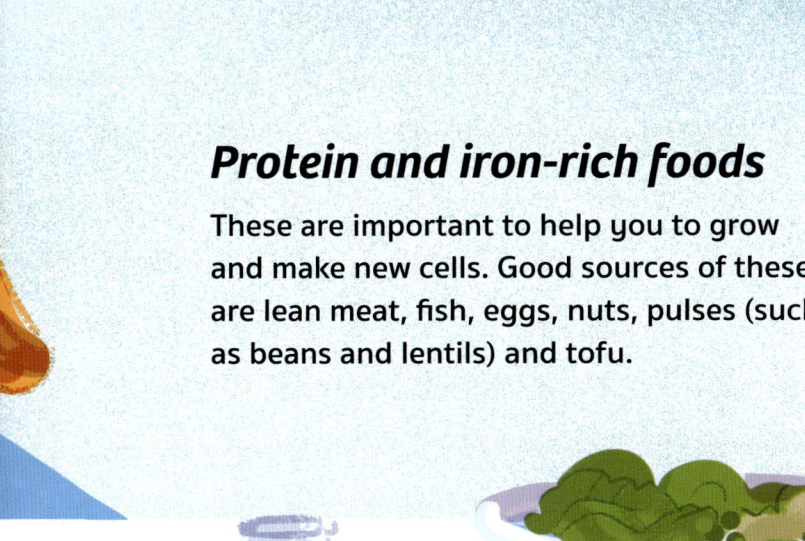

Dairy or other calcium-rich food

This is important to grow and maintain healthy bones and teeth. Milk, cheese, tofu, kefir and plain yoghurt are good sources.

Healthy fats and oils

It is important to eat some fats and oily foods, but in small amounts. These nutrients are used for building parts of cells and nerve tissue (including the brain) and producing hormones (chemical signals), plus they act as energy stores. Fats and oils are found in nuts, seeds, meats, oily fish (such as sardines), avocados and butter.

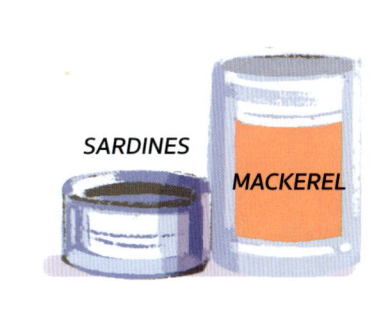

What to avoid

Try not to eat too many sugary, salty or fatty foods. These foods can provide energy, but are not very nutritious, and eating too much of them can lead to health complications. These foods include biscuits, cakes, sweets, chocolate, crisps, chips and sugary drinks.

KEEPING FIT

As with a healthy diet, regular exercise is really important in maintaining good physical and mental health. It also helps with the growth and development of your muscles, bones, movement skills, social skills and concentration. Exercise can also help you relieve stress, improve your mood and help you sleep better. So, let's get moving!

Going fast

Lots of activities and sports require bursts of activity at high speed. These bursts of speed need only be for 10 or 20 seconds, but try to go as fast as you can. After the sprint, make sure you have some time to recover and catch your breath, for example, by jogging or walking along at a slower pace. Then do it again! Lots of fun playground games involve these bursts of speed, as do sports, such as football and tennis.

Building stamina

Stamina means keeping a sustained effort at moderate intensity for a longer period of time. This should raise your heart rate and make you breathe faster during this time. Walking, jogging, skipping, dancing, swimming and cycling are all good examples of stamina training.

Getting flexible

Your joints work best if they are flexible. You can boost flexibility by doing active stretches, or activities, such as yoga or pilates. These are good exercises to do after you have been sitting still for a long time. Get into a regular routine, maybe doing them after exercising or before bedtime.

Grow strong

Gymnastics, jumping, martial arts, and throwing and catching sports are great ways to develop strength in your muscles and bones.

Other strength-developing activities you could try are sit-ups, press-ups and other bodyweight exercises. However, make sure you get a teacher to show you how to do them safely and with the best form or technique. They may also show you resistance exercises that are suitable for young people, such as how to use exercise bands, weight machines or handheld weights – but only use these under adult guidance and supervision.

A range of exercises and a balanced diet along with quality sleep can all help to keep you at a healthy weight, have lots of energy, help you concentrate, fight off infection and recover from injuries faster.

LOOKING AFTER YOUR MENTAL HEALTH

Being healthy isn't just about how physically well your body is; it is also about how you feel. This is called your mental health. Looking after your mental health can help you cope with all kinds of situations. Learning to spot signs of mental illness is just as important as understanding when your body is unwell.

What is mental illness?

Throughout our lives, we all feel a little sad, angry, anxious or overwhelmed at times. This can be for many reasons, such as school, life at home or friendships. Usually, we find a way to feel better again. But sometimes, we might find that feelings of anxiety, frustration or sadness are hard to overcome. This means these feelings remain for longer periods, and there may not be a clear reason for it. This can be a sign of mental ill health.

What now?

If you feel like you are struggling with your mental health, your first step could be to talk to someone you trust. This could be a parent or guardian, a family friend, a relative or a teacher, or you can contact a support service (see page 63). With this support, you can figure out the next steps to improve your mental wellbeing, such as making an appointment with a doctor or counsellor.

48

Good mental health

Looking after your mind doesn't mean avoiding negative feelings. It means making sure that you take care of your mental health in a way that helps you get through tough times. Excellent ways of boosting mental wellness include playing sport or exercising regularly, getting plenty of sleep, eating a balanced diet and taking care of your body.

Community and time in nature are also very important, so be sure you regularly connect with your friends and trusted adults, and make time to do things you enjoy. Limit the amount of time you spend on screens, and try to spend time outdoors.

While looking after your mental health can help a lot, it doesn't eliminate mental illness entirely. We all struggle sometimes; just make sure you talk to someone if you are feeling alone, misunderstood or feel you've lost control.

INFECTIOUS DISEASES

We all get ill from time to time. This is often because we catch an infectious disease from someone else. The diseases are caused by tiny germs, such as bacteria or viruses, which are too small to see without a microscope.

Spreading germs

Germs spread from one person to another in two main ways. Some diseases make the sick person cough and sneeze, and this sprays out germs that other people breathe in. This is how COVID-19 and flu are typically spread, as they don't live on surfaces for very long.

Other diseases, such as chickenpox and stomach bugs, are spread by touching a surface with germs on it. This may be a door handle or light switch that an ill person has touched beforehand.

This is why it is really important to wash your hands with soap and water thoroughly after going to the toilet and before preparing food.

Singing 'Happy Birthday' (or another ten-second tune) twice while washing your hands ensures that you are scrubbing for long enough.

Which germ?

Viruses: Most infections are caused by a virus. These are the smallest germs of all. They invade your body's cells and take over, making the cell create many more copies of the virus. The new viruses then set off to find the next cell to attack. Colds, chickenpox and COVID-19 are caused by viruses.

Bacteria: Sore throats and upset stomachs can be caused by bacteria. Cuts and grazes should be kept clean to stop bacterial infections.

Fungi: Itchy rashes and other skin diseases are often caused by yeast and other fungi.

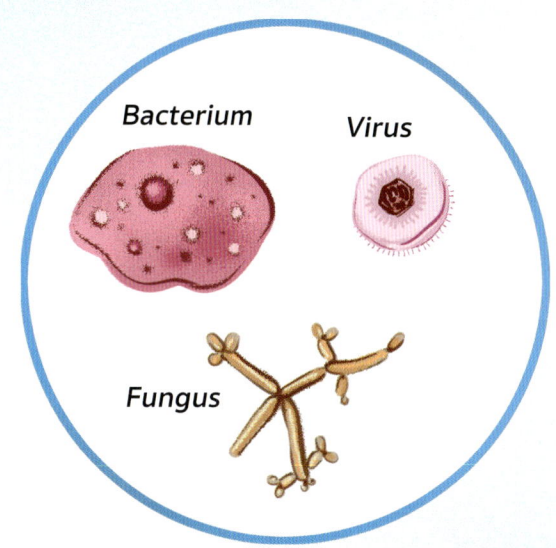

Our microbiome

The human microbiome includes non-harmful microbes that live on our skin or in our gut. Some of these bacteria, fungi and viruses actually help us with digestion and preventing infections. Amazingly, everyone has their own unique microbiome, which is shaped by their early life, diet and immune system.

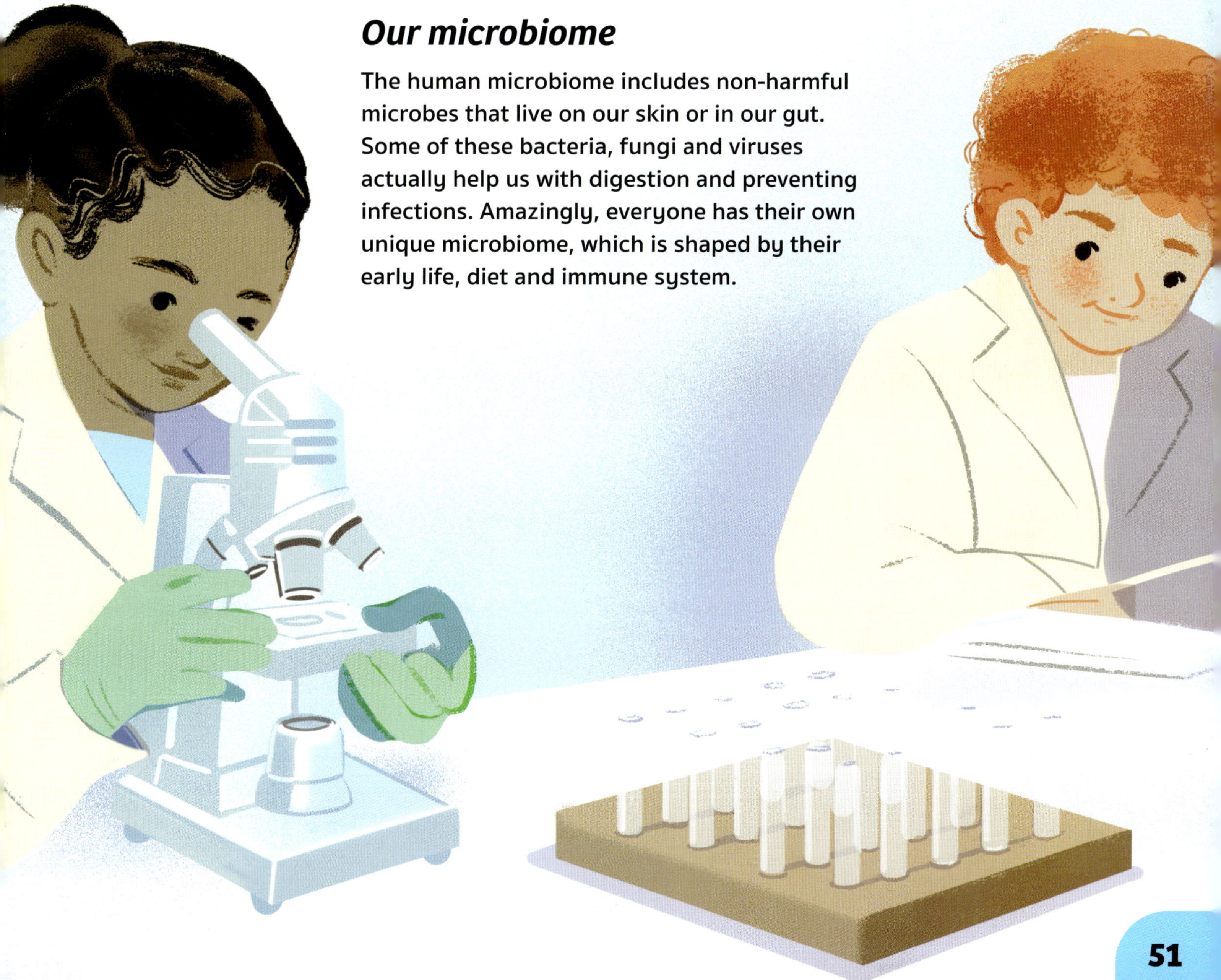

BEING ILL

When the body is under attack from germs, we do not feel very well. We are experiencing the symptoms of the disease. Some symptoms are caused by the germs, and other symptoms are caused by the body trying to get rid of the attackers.

Check the symptoms

Each illness has a typical set of symptoms. A cold usually gives us a blocked and snotty nose; with chickenpox we typically get a rash of little spots; food poisoning makes us sick.

All of these illnesses may make us feel tired, feverish or achy. This is because the body has turned on its powerful defence system to get rid of the germs.

Common symptoms

Fever: The body has turned up the heat, which helps it to destroy germs faster.

Aching: The body has released chemicals that make your nervous system more sensitive to pain. This makes you stay still and rest while your body repairs itself.

Tiredness: The body uses a lot of energy to fight infections, so you may feel sleepy.

Congestion: The body releases mucus into your nasal passages to trap germs and remove them with sneezes and coughs.

Vomiting and Diarrhoea: When the stomach and intestines are infected, they empty themselves in a hurry!

If you feel unwell or have any questions about your health, speak to a trusted adult, such as a parent, carer or teacher. If needed, they can help you seek advice from a medical professional.

KEEP CLEAN, STAY HEALTHY

It is important to keep our bodies clean. This keeps us healthy and stops us from passing on infections to others.

Washing away germs

Always wash your hands after using the toilet so that any germs in your faeces will not spread to other people. Cough and sneeze into your elbow, not your hands. If you use tissues, throw them in the bin and wash your hands. This will help to stop you from passing on germs.

Food safety

Some raw foods might have germs in them that cause food poisoning. This is why we store foods carefully, wash fresh fruits and vegetables thoroughly and cook some types of food before eating them. The cooking kills any bacteria and makes the food safe to eat.

Clean body

Keeping your body clean is called personal hygiene. Have a bath or a shower at least twice a week (if not every day). Use soap or shower gel to wash your skin, especially under your arms, between your toes and around your bottom area. Brush your teeth twice a day. As you get older, use deodorant or antiperspirant under your arms. Put on a clean pair of socks and underwear every day.

GROWING UP

You weren't born as you are now. You grew from a baby and you will continue to grow and develop until you are an adult. Even in adulthood, the human body continues to change throughout life. Just ask your grandparents!

Stages of life

After birth, there are five main stages of life.

INFANCY (up to about one year old)

The baby cannot walk or talk and needs to be looked after by an adult.

CHILDHOOD (up to about 12 years old)

This is when we learn to walk, talk, make friends and play. Early childhood starts with toddlerhood.

Middle childhood begins around seven years old, and late childhood is also called preadolescence, as it is the stage just before puberty begins.

ADOLESCENCE (lasts about five years)

In this stage of life, the body transforms from a child into an adult, as the adolescent goes through puberty (see pages 58–59).

ADULTHOOD
(from 18 years onwards)

The body's reproductive system is now fully developed. It is during this period that people might decide to have a baby (see pages 60–61).

In later adulthood, women experience menopause, which means they can no longer reproduce.

OLD AGE
(can last many years!)

The final period of our lives is often called old age, and is different for everyone.

BECOMING AN ADULT

During puberty, bodies go through a LOT of changes. It is a process that happens over many years, and while every human experiences it, it also feels different for everyone.

When? Why?

Puberty usually starts anywhere between the ages of 8 and 14 years, and everyone goes through it at a different pace. The physical changes of puberty take years as the body grows and develops into an adult body. Eventually, the body may be able to make a baby (reproduce).

How does it all start?

Some of the first changes many notice during puberty is that skin becomes oilier, which can lead to spots and greasy hair. Speaking of hair, it also starts growing in different areas of the body – the armpits, face, chest and back, as well as around the genitals (the penis and scrotum, or the vulva). No matter your sex, you may also experience swelling in the areas around the nipples. At the same time, many bodies go through a growth spurt, becoming a lot taller in a relatively small amount of time.

There's more ...

While many of the changes to hair, skin and height are similar in every body, there are also big differences between the sexes.

In female bodies, breasts grow, the vulva becomes larger and darker, and periods start. During a period (or menstruation), some blood slowly flows out of the vagina over a few days. In an adult body, periods happen about once a month, but during puberty they can be more or less frequent.

In male bodies, the voice "breaks" (becomes about an octave lower), and the penis and testicles get larger. The penis will sometimes swell and harden, which is called an erection. This can happen at any time, which can feel embarrassing, but is completely normal and often doesn't last longer than a few minutes.

Looking after yourself

Puberty also brings changes to how we feel – emotions can be far more intense and overwhelming, and they can change suddenly, without warning or obvious reason. It helps to look after ourselves by eating a balanced diet and getting regular sleep, as well as enjoying hobbies and having supportive friendships. But if feelings such as anger, anxiety and sadness feel overpowering, it is important to talk to a trusted adult.

WHERE BABIES COME FROM

When a person has gone through puberty and reached adulthood, their body is described as sexually mature. This means they may be capable of having babies in a process called reproduction.

Starts with one cell

Every person starts out as a single cell. That starting cell is made from two parts, one from each parent. The male part is a sperm cell, and it combines with an egg cell, the female part. The sperm and egg cells fuse together to make the first cell that will develop into a brand-new person. This process is called fertilisation.

Pregnancy

The new cell begins to divide and grow inside the uterus. This growing period is called pregnancy, and it lasts for about nine months (40 weeks). The tiny bundle of cells is called an embryo up to eight weeks, after which we describe it as a foetus.

It grows fast and develops all the cells, tissues, organs and organ systems that it will need. By the time it is born, the baby will be many millions of times bigger than the original cell!

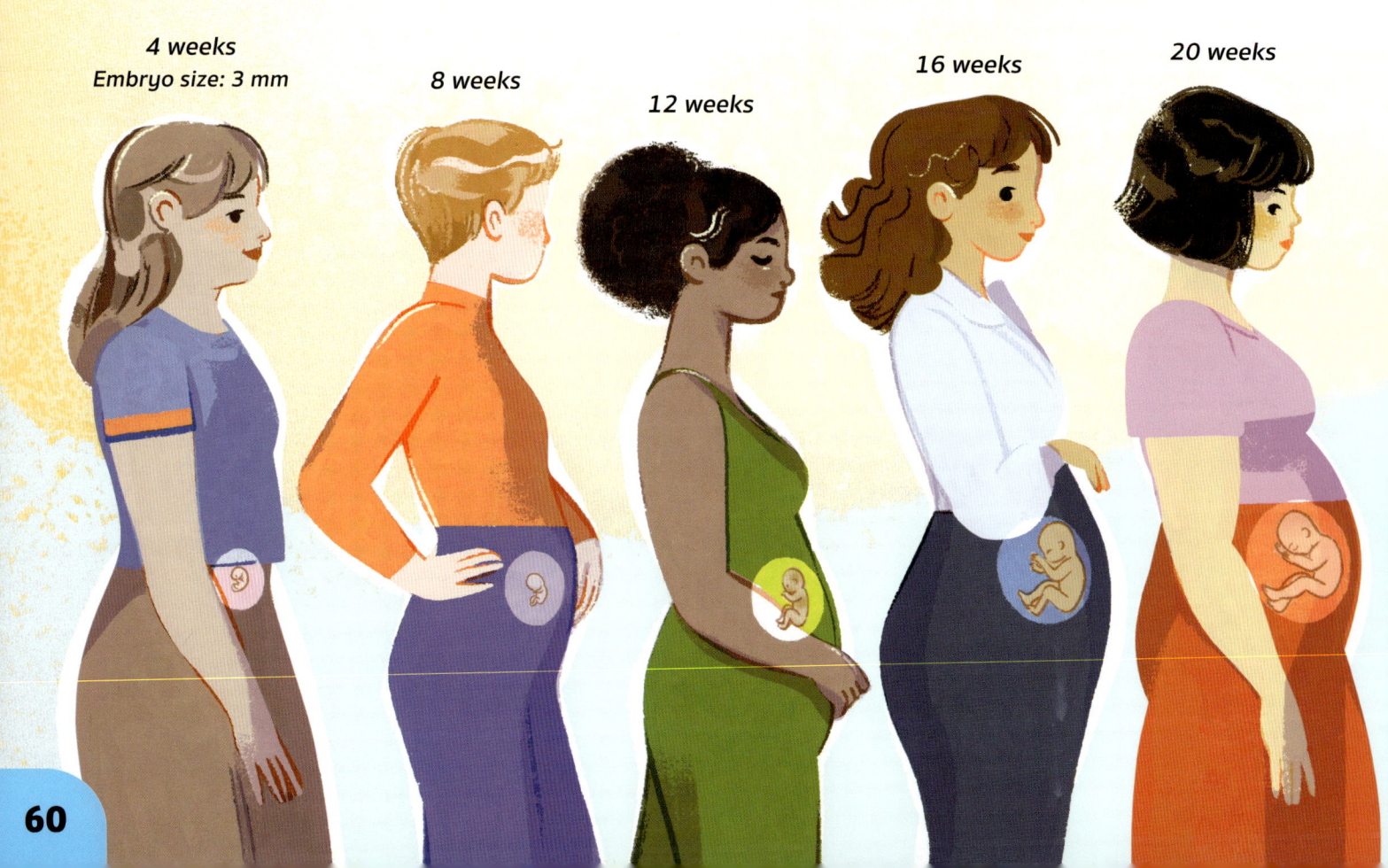

4 weeks
Embryo size: 3 mm

8 weeks

12 weeks

16 weeks

20 weeks

Nutrition for growth

The foetus gets all it needs to live and grow from the parent's blood through an organ called the placenta. This attaches to the foetus's belly button by the umbilical cord. The foetus's blood flows into the placenta to get oxygen and nutrients from the parent's body.

Birth

Many babies are born through the birth canal. The uterus opens and pushes the baby out in a process called labour. Some babies are born by Caesarean section. This is where the baby is delivered through a cut made in the birthing parent's abdomen. And so a new human is born!

The amazing human

Use this book as a springboard to learn more about all the fascinating aspects of the human body. Once you have done this, spread the knowledge by teaching others about our remarkable human bodies.

Remember, everyone's body is different in some ways, but as humans our bodies are the same in lots of ways, too. Everyone's body is amazing!

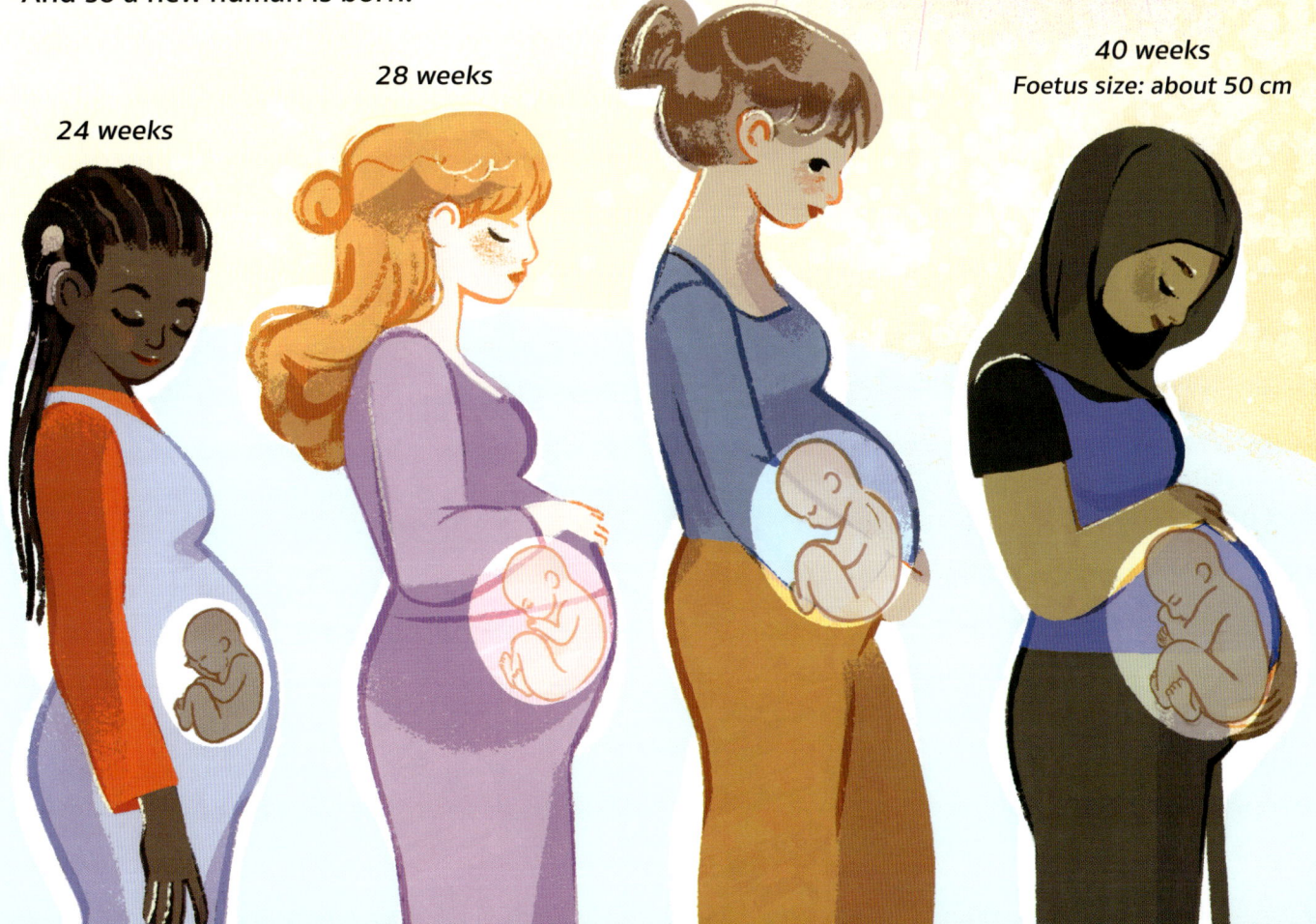

24 weeks

28 weeks

32 weeks

40 weeks
Foetus size: about 50 cm

GLOSSARY

artery: a blood vessel that carries blood away from the heart.

bacterium (many bacteria): a single-celled microorganism.

body system: a group of organs working together to do a particular job.

capillary: a thin-walled blood vessel that carries blood from arteries to veins.

cardiac: related to the heart.

cell: the basic unit of life. All organisms are made up of cells.

circulate: to travel around a system. For example, blood circulates in the body.

embryo: the new life that grows from a fertilised egg and is less than eight weeks old. The embryo eventually grows into a baby.

foetus: an embryo is known as a foetus once it has developed a full set of organs, at around eight weeks old.

genetics: the study of genes. Genes control characteristics (such as eye colour) that have been passed on by the organism's parents.

gland: an organ in the body that can release substances into the blood, such as hormones.

hormone: a chemical messenger released by a gland into the blood and carried around the body. Hormones can tell organs to carry out particular functions.

impairment: the loss or limitation of a body part or function.

intestine: a long tube-shaped organ that is part of the digestive system.

lens: a curved piece of transparent material that can change the direction of rays of light.

ligament: a band of tissue that connects bones.

microbe: an organism too small to be seen with the naked eye.

microbiome: all the microorganisms that live in an area such as the skin or digestive system.

mineral: a chemical element that is a nutrient, such as iron or magnesium. Minerals are found in many fruits and vegetables.

nerve: fibres made up of nerve cells that transfer messages to and from the brain, so the body can feel and move.

neurone: a nerve cell.

nutrient: a substance the body needs for healthy growth and functioning.

organ: a part of the body that is specialised to do particular jobs. The liver, heart and skin are all organs.

oxygenated: contains oxygen.

penis: the male sexual organ that is also used for urination.

reproduction: a process through which organisms create offspring.

scrotum: the pouch of skin that contains the testicles.

symptom: changes in the way the body works that are a sign of disease or sickness.

taste buds: tiny, bud-like sense organs on the tongue. We use them to taste what is in our mouth.

tendon: a cord of tissue that connects muscle to bone.

testicles: Reproductive organs in the male body that produce sperm. They are held in the scrotum.

tissue: when cells of the same type join together, they form tissue. Many layers of different tissue types form organs.

vagina: the female reproductive organ that is inside the body (internal). It connects the vulva to the uterus.

vein: a blood vessel that carries blood towards the heart.

virus: a non-living particle that enters a cell and can change how it functions. Viruses can cause disease, and need a host cell to be able to reproduce.

vitamin: a nutrient needed in small quantities for health (for example vitamin C).

vulva: outer (external) female reproductive organ. It is connected to the vagina.

FURTHER INFORMATION

More books to read

Taking Apart the Human Body ... to find out how it works! by Chris Oxlade and Sean O'Brien, Wayland 2025

Fact or Fake? The Truth About the Human Body by Izzi Howell, Wayland 2022

Websites

rsb.org.uk/your-expert-guide
Explore activities and learn more about the human body on this Royal Society of Biology web page!

giveusashout.org
The charity Shout offers free and confidential mental health support via text message.

youngminds.org.uk/young-person
Young Minds is a charity that offers advice for those struggling with their mental health. You can also join their campaign to provide more mental health support for young people.

INDEX

airways 17
anatomy 8

babies 19, 25, 56, 60, 61
bacteria 21, 25, 50, 51, 54
bioelectrical signals 13
biology 13
bladder 17
blood 12, 15–17, 20, 23, 26, 27, 29, 39
blood vessels 16, 17, 23, 24, 39
bones 6, 11, 14, 15, 17, 24, 39, 45–47
brain 11, 30–34, 36, 45
breathing (ventilation) 9, 12, 16, 28, 29, 46, 50

carbon dioxide 27-29
cells 6, 10, 15, 20, 27, 29, 31, 38, 40, 42, 45, 51, 60
changes in the body 6, 13, 18, 41, 56-59
chemicals 13, 21, 22, 26, 27, 35–37, 39–42, 45, 53
community 49
cytoplasm 10

defaecate (use the toilet) 23, 54
digestion 21, 22, 51
doctors 48, 53

ears 30, 31, 34
energy 20, 29, 43, 44, 53
enzymes 21
exercise 19, 46, 47, 49
eyes 16, 17, 30, 32, 33

faeces (poo) 20, 23, 54
feelings 7, 48, 49, 59
fighting illness 7, 39, 47, 52, 53
food 12, 20–25, 36, 37, 42–45, 54
food poisoning 52, 54
fungi 51

genetics 41
germs 12, 38, 50–54
giving birth 9, 16, 61

glands 39, 40
growing 7, 20, 43, 45, 46, 56–58, 60
gums 24, 25

hair 9, 13, 39–41, 58, 59
healthy diet (eating well) 7, 20, 42–47, 49, 59
heart 6, 11, 17, 26
hormones 13, 41, 45

immune system 51
infectious diseases 50, 51, 54
intestines 17, 21–23, 43, 53

joints 14, 15, 17, 18, 47

keeping clean (personal hygiene) 50, 54, 55
keeping fit 7, 46, 47

ligaments 15
liver 21, 22
lungs 6, 9, 11, 26, 29

mammals 9
mental health 46, 48, 49
mental illness 48, 49
microbes 22, 51
microbiome 51
minerals 15, 42, 44
movement 12, 14, 16, 17, 19, 20, 46
mucus 37, 53
multicellular organism 10, 11
muscles 6, 10, 11, 16–19, 26, 29, 31, 32, 36, 39, 43, 46, 47

nails 13, 40
nature (spending time in) 49
nose 30, 36, 37, 52
nutrients 20, 21, 26, 42–45, 61

offspring 13
organs 6, 11, 14, 17, 26, 27, 60, 61
organ systems 12–14, 16, 20, 22, 26, 28, 30, 42, 43, 57, 60
oxygen 26, 27, 28, 29, 61

pain 53
pancreas 21
parts of the body 8, 21–23, 26, 29, 30, 38, 58, 59
period (menstruation) 59
physiology 8
preventing infections 50, 51, 54
primates 9
puberty 56, 58–60

reproduction 57, 60, 61
respiration 29

saliva 21, 22
senses 6, 30–38
skeleton 6, 14, 15, 17
skin 9–11, 13, 17, 38–40, 55, 59
sleep 46, 47, 49, 59
sprains 15
staying healthy 7, 20, 39, 42, 43, 45–47, 49, 54
stomach 10, 11, 16, 17, 21, 22, 43, 53
symptoms (of a disease) 52, 53

teeth 21, 22, 24, 25, 36, 45, 55
tendons 17
tissues 11, 17, 24, 27, 32, 38, 45, 60
tongue 36
toxic 29

unicellular organism 10
urine (wee) 13

vertebrate animals 8, 9
viruses 36, 50, 51
vitamins 39, 42, 44

warm-blooded 9
waste (getting rid of) 13, 16, 23, 29
water 12, 23, 26, 27, 29, 39